Contents

1. **Reading** — 1
   whether ... or, vocabulary building, relative pronouns, *-ed* and *-ing* participles

2. **Reading** — 6
   vocabulary, *former* and *latter*, passive verb forms, abbreviations

3. **Writing (opinion letter), Reading** — 13
   vocabulary, phrases for advantages and disadvantages, *once* and *today*, *in addition to*

4. **Reading, Listening** — 19
   prefixes, advantages and disadvantages, vocabulary, antonyms

5. **Exam Practice** — 25
   exercise 2 reading (core), exercise 6 writing (core & extended), exercise 1 reading (extended), listening

6. **Reading, Writing (summary)** — 29
   antonyms, vocabulary, phrasal verbs

7. **Writing (note-making)** — 34
   relative pronouns, spelling (double ss), adjectives, compound nouns

8. **Writing (letter, article)** — 38
   British and American English, vocabulary

9. **Reading, Listening** — 42
   verb tenses, *irrespective of*, vocabulary

10. **Exam Practice** — 47
    exercise 2 reading (core), exercise 3 form completion (extended), exercise 7 writing (core & extended), listening

11. **Reading** — 50
    vocabulary, comparatives and superlatives

12. **Reading, Writing (summary)** — 54
    borrowed words

13. **Writing (article, letter)** — 57
    infinitive clauses, vocabulary

14 Reading, Listening   61
vocabulary, *should* and *would*, verb tenses

15 Exam Practice   66
exercise 1 reading, exercise 2 reading, exercise 4 writing (notes), exercise 5 writing (summary), exercise 6 writing (letter), exercise 7 writing (article), listening

16 Reading, Writing   73
modal auxiliary verbs, reporting verbs

17 Reading   78
however, nevertheless and *in spite of, should*, vocabulary

18 Writing (opinion article)   82
would rather, vocabulary

19 Listening   87
whether… or, vocabulary

20 Exam Practice   91
exercise 1 reading, exercise 2 reading, exercise 3 reading & writing (information transfer), exercise 4 writing (notes), exercise 5 writing (summary), exercise 6 writing (letter), exercise 7 writing (article)

Tapescript   99
Answers   107

SHEFFIELD LIBRARIES ARCHIVES & INFORMATION	
205031608	
Bertrams	23.11.05
428.24	£8.50
	ENG: Bas

Introduction

This new student workbook has been written to supplement the new edition of the coursebook, which reflects the changes in the University of Cambridge International Examinations IGCSE English as a Second Language syllabus (first examination May 2006). It is assumed that most of you who use this book will be studying English in order to promote your educational or employment prospects, and it therefore includes topics and themes relevant to these goals. You will find passages and activities based on a wide range of stimulating subjects, which we hope you will enjoy reading and discussing.

The workbook follows the same procedure as the coursebook, with each themed unit focusing on a specific aspect of the IGCSE ESL examination. However, each workbook unit also contains a section which focuses on an aspect of language, for example in unit 7 relative pronouns, and in unit 16 modal auxiliary verbs. There are also four units (units 5, 10, 15 and 20) providing examination practice, helping you to build your confidence and develop the techniques and additional skills necessary for success in the IGCSE examination.

Unit 1

Exam Focus Exercise 1 – Reading

Task 1

1. In unit 1 of the coursebook, you practised finding key words in questions. Look at the questions below and think about what the key words (or word) are in each question. You do not need to write anything yet. If you are working with someone, discuss the reasons for your choices.

   a How many methods of transport are available to reach the Isles of Scilly?
   b What is *Scillonian III*?
   c Name **four** 'treasures' of the islands.
   d Which other part of the world are the islands compared to?
   e How many people live on the Isles of Scilly?
   f What do you need to do before travelling between any of the islands?
   g On which island is the Old Wesleyan Chapel?
   h Where can you find the second oldest lighthouse in Britain?

   Write down the **type** of answer which each of the above questions requires. For example, the answer to **1a** is going to be a number because the question states '*How many* methods of transport …'.

2. Skim read the *Discover the Isles of Scilly* text and find the answers to the questions in Exercise 1. Do not write anything yet.

   Remember that in this part of the examination, you need to keep your answers **short**. In some cases you may only need to write one word, or simply a number. Some questions may require you to give more than a single piece of information, as in Question **c** in Exercise 1. When this is the case, try to write each piece of information on a separate line. The important thing is to work quickly and not to waste time repeating the question in your answer.

Discover the Isles of Scilly by air or sea

The Isles of Scilly Steamship Group provides you with two great choices to enjoy a day trip to the islands.

Whether you choose to cruise on *Scillonian III* or to fly on Skybus (the islands' own airline), and whatever time of year you visit, you will be sure to enjoy the natural beauty of the islands.

Exotic plants and wild flowers, ancient cairns and crumbling castles, sparkling white sands and an azure sea – all the treasures of the islands await you. Only 28 miles from England's Land's End, but with a real hint of the Tropics.

The Isles are populated by a community of 2,000 islanders and there are five inhabited islands to explore to make your day trip one to remember. Inter-island launches are available from St Mary's quay. Check times and tides for availability.

> St Mary's, where the airport is situated, is the largest of the islands. Hugh Town, its capital, is the commercial centre and offers a great choice of shops, restaurants and cafés. You will find the Tourist Information Centre at the Old Wesleyan Chapel in Hugh Town. Don't miss the exhibits at the museum, a walk round the Garrison and the Elizabethan fort, now known as the Star Castle Hotel. There are many walks, nature trails and safe white sand beaches.
>
> The other inhabited islands are St Martin's, Bryher, Tresco and St Agnes. On the latter is a 17th century lighthouse, the second oldest in Britain, as well as an inn and a café for refreshments. The beaches at Porth Conger and The Cove are great for swimming.

3 Which of the following would be the best response to Question **a** in Exercise 1? Why?

i   There are two methods of transport available to reach the Isles of Scilly.
ii Two.
iii There are two.
iv To reach the Isles of Scilly there are two methods of transport.

4 Write answers to the other questions in Exercise 1.

Remember that you will not be required to answer questions based on parts of the text which contain unusual vocabulary. The words *cairns* in line 5 and *launches* in line 9 are unusual, but you do not need to know what they mean in order to answer any of the questions in Exercise 1. (Note: a *cairn* is a pile of stones, often used in the past as a memorial, or to show where someone was buried; a *launch* is a type of boat, usually for transporting groups of people.)

Task 2

5 You are going to read some information taken from a leaflet about Athens International Airport. The leaflet contains information for people with special needs who may face some difficulties in the airport environment. What type of information do you think the leaflet might contain? Make a list.

Example:
Special car parking facilities

6 Here is a list of the headings contained in the leaflet. There are also two extra headings which are **not** in the leaflet. Compare the headings with your ideas from Exercise 5. Did you think of the same things? Which two headings do you think are **not** in the leaflet?

First Aid	Shopping
Free telephones and information desks	Special check-in counters and waiting areas
Parking	Special drop-off/pick-up spaces
Passport control	Toilets

7 Read the leaflet and write six of the headings from Exercise 6 in the spaces provided.

VENIZELOS AIRPORT, ATHENS –
Assistance for people with special needs

* ......

Easy access to the main airport building is provided through dedicated spaces in front of all the central entrances of both the Arrivals and Departures levels. Please note that all pavements have wheelchair ramps.

* ......

Adequate parking space in convenient locations: 36 in front of the main airport building and 101 in the airport car parks. Additionally, the long-term parking shuttle buses are equipped with ramps, and further assistance is available on request.

* ......

Depending on airline arrangements, you are welcome to check in at dedicated check-in counters next to Entrance 2 at the Departures level.

* ......

Toilets for disabled people are available in all airport areas. Signs and notices are provided in Braille.

* ......

Four First Aid rooms are available at the airport, equipped to deal with minor incidents. Emergency incidents can be handled immediately at the medical station of the Hellenic Centre of First Aid. For more information, please go to one of the Information desks, ask any of the airport employees, or use the special free telephones.

* ......

In the main airport building (close to the Information desks) there are 16 telephones with free direct connection to the airport's call centre. Disabled people have easy access to these phones; furthermore, text phones for people with hearing problems are provided.

8 The two headings which are not in the leaflet are: *Passport control* and *Shopping*. If they were in the leaflet, what information do you think they might contain? Write a few sentences for each one.

Language focus

9 What does *whether ... or* mean in the sentence below taken from the text in Task 1?

<u>Whether</u> you choose to cruise on *Scillonian III* <u>or</u> to fly on *Skybus* ... you will be sure to enjoy ...

Look at this example:
Whether we go on holiday this week or next week, it'll cost the same.

Write **five** sentences of your own to show that you understand how to use *whether ... or*.

10 All the words in the table below are taken from the two texts in this unit. Complete as many gaps in the table as possible. Remember that you may not be able to complete all the gaps.

adjective	adjective opposite	noun	verb	adverb
	ugly	beauty		
exotic				
inhabited				
available				
commercial				
		access		
				additionally
		assistance		
medical				
special				

11 Look at this sentence from the text on page 3 of your coursebook:
This is the one that sold a million in a month.

introductory phrase	noun	relative pronoun	verb phrase
This is the	*one*	*that*	*sold a million in a month.*
This/That is the ... These/Those are the ...	person/people woman/women film/films car/cars team/teams year/years reason/reasons (etc)	who when which why that where	

Use the words in the table above to write **five** sentences. There are many different possibilities. You will need to complete the final verb phrase yourself.

Example:
Those are the / reasons / why / he left the country.

12 Look at this phrase from the text on page 9 of your coursebook:
Located only minutes from the falls, the hotel has splendid views …

This information could also be written as:
The hotel is located only minutes from the falls and has splendid views …

Rewrite the following information in the same style as the phrase from your coursebook, beginning each phrase with either an *-ed* or an *-ing* participle.

  a This hotel is regarded as one of the best on the African continent and has been voted the best in Zimbabwe.

  Regarded as …

  b Your evening starts with a meal cooked by our head chef and continues with a programme of African music and dance.

  Starting with …

  c The hotel offers a full range of 5* facilities, including its own cinema, as well as a pool complex with diving boards.

  Offering …

13 Write **five** sentences of your own. Each sentence should begin with either an *-ed* or an *-ing* participle.

Vocabulary box

passport

A very literal word originating from the French 'passer', meaning 'to pass', and the word 'port' from the Latin 'portus', which refers to a point of crossing for transport and people.

Unit 2

Exam Focus Exercise 2 – Reading

Task 1

1 In unit 2 of the coursebook, you looked at information in various graphical forms (pages 12 and 15). Look at the map of Europe below, which shows how a deadly disease (plague) spread across the continent during the 14th century. What do the different shades on the map tell you?

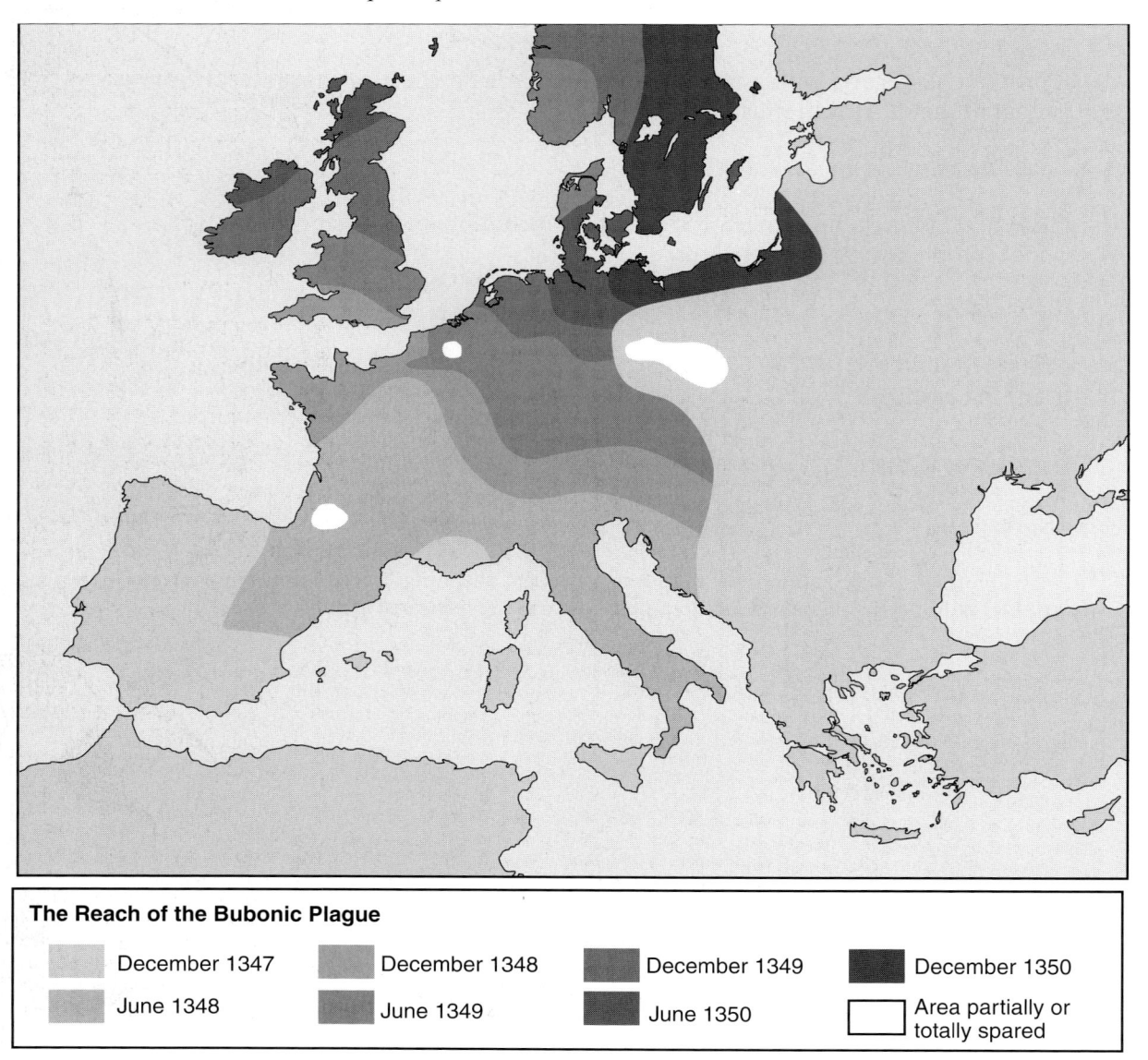

The Reach of the Bubonic Plague

December 1347	December 1348	December 1349	December 1350
June 1348	June 1349	June 1350	Area partially or totally spared

2 Match the words and phrases from the text in Column A with a suitable definition in Column B. There are two extra definitions which you do not need to use. Use your dictionary for help.

A	B
a bug (paragraph 6)	causes
b deciphered (1)	deadly
c devastated (6)	destroyed
d lethal (6)	different types
e microbe (1)	expectations
f poses (2)	germ
g resistant to (2)	infection
h rodents (3)	made sense of
i strains (2)	rats
j wiped out (4)	removed
	security
	unaffected by

3 Skim the text. Find the words from Column A in Exercise 2. Do the definitions you chose from Column B make sense?

SCIENTISTS DECIPHER DNA CODE OF PLAGUE
(BY TIM RADFORD, SCIENCE EDITOR)

(1) Scientists have deciphered the entire genetic code of one of the great diseases of mankind – the plague. The 465 million 'letters' of the DNA of a bacterium (or microbe) called 'Yersinia pestis' could begin to answer questions about a disease that changed history at least three times – and could do so again.

(2) The recent identification of strains of plague resistant to drugs, and the possibility of using the microbe 'yersinia pestis' as a chemical weapon in a war, mean that plague still poses a threat to humans.

(3) Plague affected Europe in the 6th and 8th centuries, as well as repeatedly between the 14th and 18th centuries (when it was known as the 'Black Death'), and it continues to cause problems in the 21st century. It survives in groups of rodents and is carried to humans by the bite of an infected insect. Plague is not the first killer disease to be identified and deciphered – scientists already have the genetic codes for cholera, malaria, leprosy, meningitis and many others. But plague has been the most dramatic killer of all.

(4) The Black Death is believed to have wiped out one third of Europe's population as it spread westwards from the Far East across the continent in the 14th century. The World Health Organisation receives reports of up to 3,000 infections each year. The deadly bacterium lives in populations of rats in Asia and the western United States of America, and from time to time it spreads to city rats in other parts of the world.

(5) The strain used to decipher the plague code came from a vet who died in 1992 after a cat with pneumonic plague sneezed on him. He was trying to rescue the cat from underneath a house at the time. Many people do not realise that plague is still with us, although it is not nearly as common as it used to be.

(6) The microbe probably began in the form of a stomach infection and developed into something much more lethal around 1,500 years ago. It has adopted a different lifestyle in a remarkably short space of time, changing basically from a stomach bug to a killer disease that has devastated the world.

(7) The DNA code of plague will help researchers looking for new drugs and medicines. One medicine is already being tested. Plague has also been proposed as a possible chemical weapon.

(8) The Facts of Death

Plague lives in two forms: the lethal pneumonic variety, spread by coughing and sneezing; the other is the bubonic variety, which exists mostly in America, Africa and Asia. This latter variety was identified in 1894 by a scientist called Alexandre Yersin, who originally named it 'Pasteuralla pestis' after his teacher, Louis Pasteur. The last big outbreak of pneumonic plague, in India in 1992, killed 855 people. The last outbreak in London was the Great Plague of 1665.

Adapted from *The Guardian*, p. 5, Tim Radford, 04/10/01

4 Read the following questions and find the key word or words in each one. You do not need to write anything yet.

    a What is the name of the bacterium whose code has been deciphered?
    b Apart from being resistant to drugs, what other threat does the bacterium pose to humans?
    c When did the plague first affect Europe?
    d Where does modern plague survive today and how is it transferred to humans?
    e List **four** other diseases whose genetic codes have been deciphered by scientists.
    f What effect did the 'Black Death' have on Europe in the 14th century?
    g In which direction did the plague travel across Europe in the 14th century?
    h How was the vet infected with pneumonic plague?
    i What form did the plague probably take 1,500 years ago?
    j Name the **two** varieties of plague known to scientists.
    k Why was bubonic plague originally called 'Pasteuralla pestis'?
    l When and where were 855 people killed by pneumonic plague?

5 Skim the text again and try to find the key words you identified in the questions in Exercise 4.

6 Write your answers to the questions in Exercise 4. Remember to keep your answers as brief as possible, but include all the necessary information.

Task 2

7 You are going to read an article about an archaeological discovery in Greece. The text contains some vocabulary which you may not know. Here are 11 words and phrases which have been removed from the text. Use your dictionary to check the meaning of each one. Do not look at the text yet. Write down the meanings of each word.

    a exploits   **e** myths   **i** stumbled across
    b mundane   **f** painstaking   **j** determination
    c excavating   **g** settlement   **k** perplexed
    d composite   **h** quest

8 Here are the meanings (not in the right order) which fit the words and phrases in Exercise 7. Check your answers.

    strength   digging out   legends
    careful   worried   routine
    community   discovered   activities
    complex   expedition

Now use these 'meanings' to complete the grid on page 9. The letters in the shaded area will reveal an important word from the text.

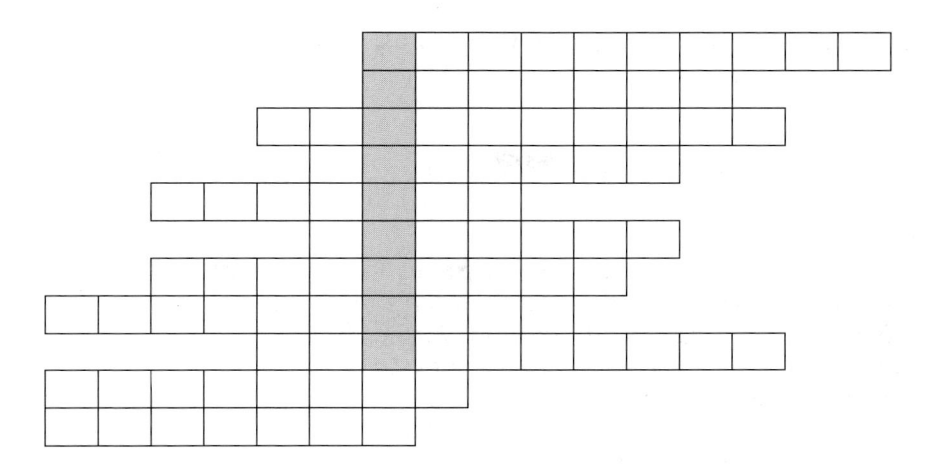

9 Skim the text. Use the words from Exercise 7 to complete each gap. Make sure you use the context (the phrases before and after each gap) to help you.

GOLDEN LEGEND UNEARTHED IN GREECE

High in the foothills of central Greece evidence is emerging that may explain one of the world's longest-lasting (1) … . Archaeologists are (2) … the remains of what they believe is ancient Iolcus, the city which Jason and the Argonauts departed from to find the Golden Fleece.

Located on a former vegetable field in the Thessalian village of Dimini, the excavation lies below an important neolithic (3) … from more than 7,000 years ago, long before the age of the Greek heroes. This particular excavation site also has a 'tholos': a beehive-shaped tomb (a place for burying people), which is associated with Mycenaean culture 3,200 to 3,600 years ago.

Vasso Adrimi discovered the large Mycenaean settlement in central Greece nearly 25 years ago. But linking reality to legend was no easy business. 'I spent two months examining the site and was most (4) … ,' she says. 'It came as a shock, a very big shock, when my professor linked the site to the two Mycenean royal 'tholos' tombs we also have here. He said: "Keep going, I have no doubt that this is the ancient Mycenean city of Iolcus. You have (5) … the find of your life,"' says Ms Adrimi, who kept going with great (6) … .

Now, assisted by modern technology, she has pieced together enough evidence to suggest that the Jason legend may have been based on the (7) … of a seafaring people who sailed on the Black Sea.

'We may never know who Jason was, or if he ever existed, but I think it is safe to say the myth of the Argonauts is the product of historical memory, dressed up with lots of dramatic fiction,' she says.

Ms Adrimi belongs to a small group in Greece who believe in 'breaking the barrier of time' by studying even the most (8) … aspects of ancient life. Hers is a (9) … method of enquiry, which is not interested in the glory that goes in hand with a more sensational type of archaeological find.

The claim of identifying Iolcus is based on a (10) … picture of life around a palace, but it was the discovery of moulds for making jewellery, weapons and tools that set her thinking. 'The raw materials, like gold, obviously needed to be obtained from somewhere – maybe the myth of the Argonauts was inspired by the memory of the (11) … to bring them back.'

Adapted from *The Guardian Weekly*, p. 22, Helena Smith, 11–17/10/01

10 Read the questions and find the key word or words in each one.

    a What have archaeologists found in central Greece?
    b What is the shape of a 'tholos'?
    c When was the community first discovered?
    d How did Vasso Adrimi feel when she examined the site?
    e Who encouraged Vasso in her search?
    f What has helped Ms Adrimi to put together the evidence she needs?
    g What does she think the legend of Jason may be based on?
    h Name **three** items made using the moulds which Ms Adrimi found.

11 Now write the answers to the questions in Exercise 10.

Language focus

12 Read the phrases in Column A. Which words or phrases from Column B match the the phrases in Column A? Some words and phrases in Column B cannot be used. The phrases in Column A will match with either one or two words or phrases.

Column A	Column B
a made into an understandable language	deadly
b caused great destruction	deciphered
c causing death	destroyed
d the word originates from Greek and means 'small life'	devastated
e sits for a photograph	different types
f hostile to	germ
g animals which often carry disease	lethal
h stretches something tightly	made sense of
i taken off	microbe
	poses
	rats
	removed
	resistant to
	rodents
	strains
	unaffected by
	wiped out

    a ... ... (2 words or phrases)   **d** ... (1)   **g** ... ... (2)
    b ... ... (2)   **e** ... (1)   **h** ... (1)
    c ... ... (2)   **f** ... (1)   **i** ... (1)

13 Choose **five** words or phrases from Exercise 12 and use them in sentences of your own.

Example:
His writing was so awful that she <u>made</u> no <u>sense of</u> it.

14 What does *latter* mean in the sentence below taken from Task 1, paragraph 8?

This <u>latter</u> variety was identified…

Look at these examples:
1 *Plague lives in two forms: the pneumonic and the bubonic. The <u>former</u> is spread by coughing; the <u>latter</u> is found in Asia.*
2 *There are two main sources of water: underground rivers and man-made dams. The <u>former</u> can be found all over the island while the <u>latter</u> have been built in areas of high rainfall.*

Write **five** sentences of your own to show that you understand how to use *former* and *latter*.

15 The two texts in this unit refer to events which happened long ago. Often these types of text use the passive form of the verb (*to be* + past participle).

Examples:
1 *The Black Death <u>is believed</u> to have happened in the 14th century.*
2 *The claim of identifying Iolcus <u>is based</u> on a …*

Use the words and phrases in the table below to write meaningful sentences. Put each verb into its correct passive form. Don't worry if you are not sure about the correct dates!

a The Solar System (form)	by dinosaurs	in 1961
b The planet Earth (dominate)	by Marconi	in the 16th century
c Copper and gold (use)	to Europe by rats	in the 18th century
d The bubonic plague (bring)	by only 5 million people worldwide	in 1894
e English (speak)	to Europe from Latin America	in 2004
f Rubber (bring)	in Athens, Greece,	around 1346
g The radio (invent)	into space	during the Bronze Age
h The first man, Yuri Gagarin, (launch)	by man	about 4,600 million years ago
i The Olympic Games (hold)	by gases	about 235 million years ago

16 In this unit you have seen these abbreviations: IGCSE, DNA. What do they stand for?

IGCSE   International General Certificate of Secondary Education
DNA   deoxyribonucleic acid

Now find what these abbreviations stand for, and write them in full. Use your dictionary for help.

a WHO
b BBC
c DVD
d VCR
e UNICEF
f NATO
g SMS
h UFO

Vocabulary box

volcanoes

Volcanoes are named after Vulcan, the Roman god of fire. Volcanoes are categorised into three stages: *dormant*, which comes from the Latin 'dormire' meaning 'to sleep'; *active*, which comes from the Latin 'activus' and means 'having physical movement'; *extinct*, which is from the Latin 'extinctus' and means 'no longer burning'.

Unit 3

Exam Focus Exercise 6 – Writing

Task 1

1. You are going to read a text about veganism. Before you read, look at these words and phrases from the text. Match each one with a suitable definition in the opposite column. Use your dictionary for help.

Words and phrases	Definition
absorption (paragraph 10)	developed or coming from something else
adequate (5)	enough, sufficient
chronic (6)	meat from birds such as chicken and ducks
conform to (6)	milk, cheese, butter, etc.
dairy foods ((1)	not containing
derived from (1)	not treating animals and people in a cruel way
free of (6)	obey a rule
humane (3)	obeying all the rules
poultry (1)	only a little
sparingly (6)	process where something takes in something else
strict (5)	continuing for a long time

2. These sentences and phrases are taken from the text. Use the words from Exercise 1 to complete the gaps.

   a Vegetarians do not eat meat, fish, or …… .
   b Vegans do not use other animal products, such as honey, eggs and …… .
   c Cosmetics and soaps are …… animal products.
   d Many vegans choose this lifestyle to promote a more …… and caring world.
   e It is easy for a vegan diet to meet the recommendations for protein as long as calorie intake is …… .
   f …… protein planning or combining is not necessary.
   g Vegan diets are …… cholesterol and are generally low in fat.
   h Thus eating a vegan diet makes it easy to …… recommendations given to reduce the risk of major …… diseases such as cancer.
   i High-fat foods, which should be used ……, include oils and nuts.
   j Iron …… is increased markedly by eating foods containing vitamin C.

3. Skim the text. Find the words and phrases from Exercise 1.

4 There are eleven paragraphs in the text. Each paragraph has a heading. Read the headings below and decide which one goes with each paragraph.

Calcium	Iron	What is a vegan?
Caring	Protein	Why veganism?
Fat	Vegan nutrition	Zinc
For more information	Vitamin D	

Why not become a vegan?

(1) _____
Vegetarians do not eat meat, fish or poultry. Vegans, in addition to being vegetarian, do not use other animal products, such as honey, eggs and dairy foods, nor animal by-products, for example leather, fur, silk, wool, cosmetics and soaps derived from animal products.

(2) _____
People choose to be vegan for health, environmental and/or ethical reasons. For example, some vegans feel that by consuming eggs and dairy products, the meat industry is promoted. That is, once dairy cows or egg-laying chickens are too old to be productive, they are often sold as meat; and since male calves do not produce milk, they are usually raised for veal or other meat products. Some people avoid these items because of the conditions associated with their production.

(3) _____
Many vegans choose this lifestyle to promote a more humane and caring world. They know that they are not perfect, but believe that they have a responsibility to try to do their best, while not being judgemental of others.

(4) _____
The key to a nutritionally sound vegan diet is variety. A healthy and varied vegan diet includes fruits, vegetables, plenty of leafy greens, whole grain products, nuts, seeds and legumes.

(5) _____
It is very easy for a vegan diet to meet the recommendations for protein as long as calorie intake is adequate. Strict protein planning or combining is not necessary. The key is to eat a varied diet. Almost all foods, except for sugar and fats, are good sources of protein. Vegan sources include: potatoes, whole wheat bread, rice, broccoli, spinach, almonds, peas, chickpeas, peanut butter, tofu, soy milk, lentils, kale. For example, if part of a day's menu included the following foods, you would meet the Recommended Dietary Allowance (RDA) for protein for an adult male: 1 cup oatmeal, 1 cup soy milk, 2 slices whole wheat bread, 1 bagel, 2 tablespoons peanut butter, 1 cup vegetarian baked beans, 5 ounces tofu, 2 tablespoons almonds, 1 cup broccoli and 1 cup brown rice.

(6) _____
Vegan diets are free of cholesterol and are generally low in fat. Thus eating a vegan diet makes it easy to conform to recommendations given to reduce the risk of major chronic diseases such as heart disease and cancer. High-fat foods, which should be used sparingly, include oils, margarine, nuts, nut butters, seed butters, avocado and coconut.

(7) _____
Vitamin D is not found in the vegan diet but can be made by humans with at least ten to fifteen minutes of summer sun on the hands and face two to three times a week. This is recommended for adults so that vitamin D production can occur.

(8) _____
Calcium, needed for strong bones, is found in dark green vegetables, tofu processed with calcium sulfate, and many other foods commonly eaten by vegans. Calcium requirements for those on lower protein, plant-based diets may be somewhat lower than requirements for those eating a higher protein, flesh-based diet. However, it is important for vegans to eat foods high in calcium and/or use a vegan calcium supplement every day.

(9) _____
Vegan diets can provide zinc at levels close to or even higher than the RDA. Zinc is found in grains, legumes and nuts.

(10) _____
Dried beans and dark green vegetables are especially good sources of iron (see chart), better on a per calorie basis than meat. Iron absorption is increased markedly by eating foods containing vitamin C along with foods containing iron.

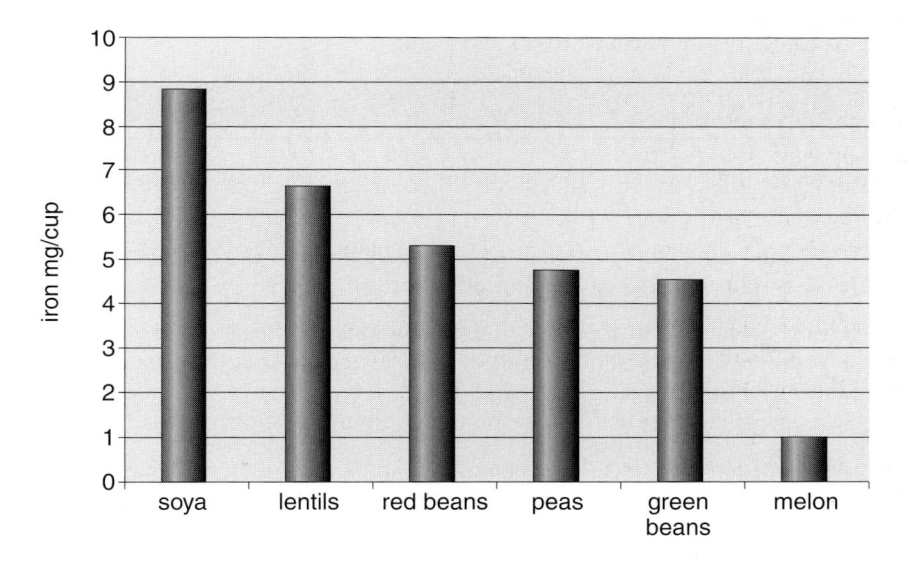

(11) _____
Order *Simply Vegan* for a complete discussion of vegan nutrition plus 160 quick and easy recipes. This excellent resource contains over 160 vegan recipes that can be prepared quickly. An extensive vegan nutrition section by Reed Mangels, Ph.D., R.D., covers topics such as protein, fat, calcium, iron, vitamin B12, pregnancy and the vegan diet, feeding vegan kids, weight gain, weight loss, and a nutrition glossary. Also featured are sample menus and meal plans. *Simply Vegan* is more than a cookbook. An additional section on shopping by mail tells you where to find vegan clothes, non-leather shoes, cosmetics, household products and books.

Adapted from http://www.vrg.org/nutshell/vegan.htm 18/01/04

5 In unit 3 of the coursebook you reviewed phrases to express opinion. Imagine that your friend is thinking of becoming a vegan. Write an informal letter to her/him expressing your opinion about veganism. Write between 150 and 200 words and include in your letter:

– the kind of people who become vegans
– the products that vegans eat and use
– why you think veganism would / would not suit your friend.

Task 2

6 You are going to read a passage about obesity. First, look at these questions:

  a What does *obesity* mean? Use your dictionary for help.
  b What do you think causes obesity?
  c In which countries do most people suffer from obesity?
  d Do you think the levels of obesity are changing? Why?

7 Which of these words do you think will appear in the text? Write down your choices. Try to give reasons for your choices. Use your dictionary for help.

| businessmen | teenagers | fashion | friends | smoking | gym | advertising |
| Asia | tiger | bomb | chocolate | carbohydrate | prosperity | |

8 Skim the text to check your choices in Exercise 7.

Obesity – fat of the land

The government worries that it should do something to change the way people eat. But diets are already changing.

Given mankind's need to worry, it is not surprising that the diseases of prosperity – stress, depression and, increasingly, obesity, get a lot of attention.

(1) Obesity is a serious problem as it increases the risk of diabetes, heart disease and cancer. It is not clear what governments can do about it and evidence suggests that the idea of imposing taxes on foods is not necessarily the answer. In Sweden, where advertising to young people is already banned, children are as overweight as they are in any comparable country.

(2) Furthermore, it is not obvious that the problem will worsen. Shoppers' behaviour suggests the opposite. It is not just the flight from carbohydrates; there is a broader shift going on.

(3) Companies are edging away from fattening foods. Five years ago, chocolate made up 80% of sales in a world-leading company; now that is down to half. Five years ago 85% of drinks sales were sweet, fizzy stuff. That's down to 56%. The rest is mostly juice. Diet drinks – which make up a third of the sales of fizzy drinks – are growing at 5% a year, while sales of the fattening stuff are static.

(4) Supermarkets say that people are buying healthier foods. Lower calorie ranges grew by 12% in 2003, twice the growth in overall sales. Sales of fruit and vegetables are growing faster than overall sales, too. Cafés and restaurants also report an increase in healthy eating. A sandwich store says that sales of salads grew by 63% last year.

(5) But it isn't just eating too much fatty stuff that makes people fat. It's laziness, too. That may be changing. According to a market-research company, there were 3.8m members of private gyms last year, up from 2.2m in 1998. The average man got thinner in 2002.

(6) Obesity is also seen as a class issue, and where the rich lead, the poor tend to follow – partly because the poor get richer over time, and partly because health messages tend to reach the better-educated first and the worse-educated later. That's what has been happening with smoking, a habit the rich gave up years ago and the poor are now stubbing out too. With younger consumers peer pressure tends to have more impact on teenagers than any amount of government intervention.

Adapted from *The Economist*, 6–12/03/04

9 Match the headings below to the paragraphs in the text on the previous page.

  a Class and trends
  b Health dangers of obesity
  c Statistics on the sales of fattening foods
  d Not just what you eat
  e Shoppers' habits
  f Sales of healthier products

10 Here are some notes based on each heading from Exercise 9. Write a passage of about 150–200 words using the notes to guide you. Make sure you use the notes in the same order as the information appears in the text.

- Class and trends
  the poor follow the rich / smoking / peer pressure and government intervention
- Health dangers of obesity
  diseases / food taxes / Sweden
- Statistics on the sales of fattening foods
  chocolate sales / drinks
- Not just what you eat
  lifestyles / fitness clubs
- Shoppers' habits
  carbohydrates
- Sales of healthier products
  low calorie foods / fruit and vegetables / cafés and restaurants

Language focus

11 In this unit you have seen a lot of vocabulary connected with food. Find **thirteen** food words hidden in the box below.

p	o	i	u	y	t	k	r	e	p	w	q
l	s	p	a	g	h	e	t	t	i	k	j
h	a	g	f	d	a	b	s	a	z	m	n
b	n	v	c	r	m	a	x	z	z	b	q
w	d	e	r	i	b	b	t	y	a	e	u
i	w	o	p	c	u	r	r	y	m	a	a
m	i	l	k	e	r	s	d	f	e	n	g
h	c	j	k	l	g	o	u	l	a	s	h
z	h	h	o	n	e	y	x	c	t	v	b
n	m	p	l	m	r	n	j	i	u	t	f

Unit 3   17

12 There are various phrases which you can use to write about advantages and disadvantages. Add more phrases to the lists below.

advantages	disadvantages
On the plus side …	*Another drawback is …*

13 In the *Shellfish in Oman* text on page 26 in your coursebook, look at how the adverbs *once* and *today* are used:
<u>Once</u>, *abalone shellfish were brought to the surface …*
<u>Today</u>, *the shellfish are caught for …*.

Here, *once* means 'at some stage in the past', and *today* means 'at the present time'.

Write **eight** sentences which show you can correctly use these two adverbs.

14 Look at this sentence from the text about veganism in this unit of your workbook.

Vegans, <u>in addition to</u> being vegetarian, do not use other animal products.

We use *in addition to* to add information to the subject, or to join two or more pieces of information together. *In addition to* can be at the start of or within a sentence.

Examples:
People choose to be vegan for health, environmental and/or ethical reasons.
People, <u>in addition to</u> choosing to be vegan for health reasons, do so for environmental and/or ethical reasons.
<u>In addition to</u> *choosing to be vegan for health reasons, people do so for environmental and/or ethical reasons.*

Rewrite the following information using *in addition to*:

a Many vegans choose this lifestyle to promote a more humane and caring world, as well as believing that they have a responsibility to try to do their best.
b A healthy and varied vegan diet includes fruits, vegetables and plenty of leafy greens, as well as whole grain products, nuts, seeds and legumes.
c Vegan diets are free of cholesterol and are generally low in fat.
d Calcium is found in dark green vegetables and many other foods commonly eaten by vegans.
e *Simply Vegan* contains a complete discussion of vegan nutrition plus 160 quick and easy recipes.

Vocabulary box

restaurant

This word comes from the French 'restaurer', meaning 'to restore'. The public dining room that came ultimately to be known as the restaurant originated in France, especially during the Napoleonic era.

Unit 4

Exam Focus – Reading, Listening

Task 1

1 You are going to read an Internet article about how advertising can have an effect on young people. There are five sections in the article. Each section has a heading:

1 Children's understanding of advertising
2 Media literacy
3 Benefits of advertising to children
4 Advertising does not encourage children to ask for more
5 Advertising does not influence diet

In which of the five sections do you think you are more likely to find the following **nine** phrases? Try to give reasons for your choices.

a ... they comprehend that advertising is there to sell to them.
b Advertisements also may not encourage eating or drinking near bedtime.
c Banning advertising during children's programming would not insulate children from commercial messages ...
d By the age of 7 or 8 most children are fully aware of the persuasive nature of advertising ...
e Children have always asked their parents for things ...
f Advertising of snack foods directed at children is much greater than that of fruit and vegetables.
g Children have to develop the ability to make critical comparisons ...
h Further restrictions on advertising would affect the choice and quality of programming for children ...
i If advertising was banned or restricted, commercial broadcasters would reduce or cease their investment in original programme production.

2 Find words in the text which have a similar meaning to the following. Write them down. Use your dictionary for help.

a effect (section 1)
b purpose (1)
c convincing (1)
d buyers (1)
e protect (2)
f connection (3)
g income (3)
h spending (3)
i stopped (3)
j large (3)
k asking repeatedly (4)
l pressure (5)
m very clear (5)

Unit 4   19

Children and advertising

(1) **Children's understanding of advertising**
Children enjoy and remember advertisements but this does not necessarily mean that they have an impact on their behaviour. Research conducted by Dr Brian Young has shown that children do understand the difference between advertising and editorial or programme content from the age of 3. From around the age of 5 children also begin to understand the commercial intent of advertising – i.e. that it is trying to sell you something. By the age of 7 or 8 most children are fully aware of the persuasive nature of advertising and have an understanding of it. Full understanding increases with age, but before they are acting independently as purchasers, they comprehend that advertising is there to sell to them.

(2) **Media literacy**
Children today are exposed to a wider range of influences, cultures and media than any other generation. Banning advertising during children's programming would not insulate children from commercial messages – they would still see products they like advertised in a positive light in shop windows – should this also be restricted?

Understanding the role of advertising and marketing is an essential part of growing up and becoming a citizen in a free market democracy. Children have to develop the ability to make critical comparisons and informed decisions.

(3) **Benefits of advertising to children**
With worries for safety outside, children's play increasingly takes place within the home. Computer games, television and the internet are today the main sources of children's entertainment. Further restrictions on advertising would affect the choice and quality of programming for children, forcing them to watch programmes intended for adults instead.

There is a direct correlation between advertising revenue generated during children's programme hours and expenditure on children's programming. If advertising was banned or restricted, commercial broadcasters would reduce or cease their investment in original programme production. This has happened in Sweden, where commercial broadcasters do not exceed five hours a week minimum of children's programming. It is also borne out in Greece, where a ban on toy advertising since 1994 has led to a 40% decline in children's programme investment. Some children-only channels would cease to exist at all. Thus there would be a substantial reduction in the choice and quality of programmes and television channels available to children.

(4) **Advertising does not encourage children to ask for more**
In research carried out in 1999, only 14% of parents cited television advertising as one of the top five influences on their children. Other research conducted in the same year in Sweden found that despite a ban on all TV advertising to under 12 year olds, more Swedish adults felt that pestering was a problem (9%) compared to Spanish adults (7%). Children have always asked their parents for things, but laws do not permit advertisements to encourage this.

(5) **Advertising does not influence diet**
Advertising of snack foods directed at children is much greater than that of fruit and vegetables. Some groups claim this relationship becomes reflected in children's diets, causing diet-related problems.

However, being overweight is a result of the imbalance between energy in and energy out. Whereas foods with high calorie content have fallen in the last decade, levels of physical activity among children have declined further. For example, since 1986, the number of walking trips made by young people has fallen by 17% for those aged between 5 and 10 years and by 29% for those aged 11 to 15 years. Problems of overweight are likely to be a product of falling levels of exercise.

Major influences on children's diets do not include advertising, particularly among younger children, who do not make their own purchasing or dietary decisions. In *Recent Research into Children's Dietary Choices* (1994), Dr Peter Stratton found that advertising is not considered a major influence on children's diets and parents do not believe that it has encouraged children to pester adults for specific foods. He quantified TV advertising as influencing only 5% of food choices and 9th on the list of influences after family and friends.

Laws about advertising practice are explicit about not encouraging children to eat frequently throughout the day or replace meals with snacks. Advertisements also may not encourage eating or drinking near bedtime.

Adapted from http://www.fau.org.uk/ 01/02/04

3 Decide if the following statements about the text you have read are true or false.

   a Children do not understand the difference between advertising and normal programme content from an early age.
   b Before children start to buy things, they understand the real purpose of advertising is to make them spend money.
   c Stopping advertising during children's programmes would not protect them from advertisers' messages.
   d Restrictions on advertising would improve the quality of children's programmes.
   e Most parents do not believe that television advertising affects their children.
   f There is more advertising of fruit and vegetables than snack foods.
   g Children take part in less physical activity than they did ten years ago.
   h Overweight problems are a result of too many snack foods rather than not enough physical exercise.

Task 2

4 You are going to listen to a spokesperson from the FAU (Food Advertising Unit) being interviewed about the effects of advertising on children. Before you listen, look at some of the questions which the interviewer asks the spokesperson. What do you think the answers might be?

   a What do parents and adults think about advertising to children?
   b I understand some research has been carried out to determine what parents think about this. What does the research tell us?
   c But do parents want stricter controls over advertising aimed at children?
   d So, in general then, do parents and adults see advertising to children as a major problem?
   e Does advertising have any effect on diet-related problems?
   f Is there any scientific evidence of the extent of advertising's influence on food choice?

Now look at some possible responses to the questions and decide which response could match each question.

i   Most certainly, although it is difficult to come to any conclusions because the facts seem to contradict themselves
ii Norway and Belgium have three or four times less food advertisements per hour on average than Germany, Denmark, Finland and the Netherlands, yet suffer from higher levels of obesity.
iii Parents see no need for additional rules or laws regarding advertising.
iv Some parents believe that advertising manipulates their children into wanting things they don't need …
v   According to a report on the Promotion of Food to Children, published in 2001, there is actually little public concern over food advertising.
vi There is general agreement that advertising is not one of the major influences on children.

5   Listen to the interview and complete the notes below. Track 1

1 Some parents believe advertising makes their children want things they don't need, whilst others believe advertising helps them to ……… their children will like.
2 Children understand that TV commercials make them want products and this understanding is clear, even amongst the ……… , the youngest children in the group discussions.
3 In a study in 2000, commissioned by the Advertising Education Forum, ……… did not mention TV advertising as one of the five major influences on their choice of food.
4 In the UK, only 5% mentioned advertising as an influence, and in Denmark 41%. In Sweden, where ……… , 11% of parents felt it to be a major influence.
5 There is general agreement that advertising is not ……… on children and that broadly parents, brothers and sisters, friends and school are more powerful.
6 Norway and Belgium have ……… times less food advertisements per hour on average than Germany, Denmark, Finland and the Netherlands.
7 There is no reason to assume that advertising will ……… affect a child's dietary health. It can influence it, but this influence could just as easily be positive as negative.
8 Restricting advertising during children's programming would not protect them from commercial messages. Understanding the role of marketing and developing the ability to make ……… is an essential part of growing up and becoming a citizen in a free market democracy.

Language focus

6 The words *contradict* and *conclusion* are used in the interview. Each word begins with a different prefix: *contra-* and *con-*. What do these prefixes mean? Use your dictionary for help.

7 Here are some other prefixes used in this unit. Match them to their meaning. Use your dictionary for help.

in-	thoroughly, very; through
ex-	shows a negative, an opposite; in, on
en-	under
pro-	former and still living; out, from
per-	in favour of
ad-	to cause to become; make
sub-	in the direction of; towards, to

Now find words from the *Children and advertising* text that begin with the prefixes in the first column:

prefix	words from text	your words
con-	conclusion	conduct, convey
contra-	contradict	contraband, contrast
in-		
ex-		
en-		
pro-		
per-		
ad-		
sub-		

8 You found out in the unit that an advantage of advertising to children is that:
It increases the quantity of children's programmes.

A disadvantage of advertising to children is that:
It could encourage children to eat more snack food.

Now write one advantage and one disadvantage for each of the following statements. Use some of the advantages and disadvantages phrases you thought of in unit 3 Exercise 12.

  a Children normally have to go to school until the age of 16.
  b Teenagers are normally not allowed to work full-time until they are 16.
  c The year is divided into four seasons: autumn, winter, spring and summer.
  d More and more families have a computer in their home.
  e Children have to do sports at school.

9 Complete this chart. All the words have been taken from this unit. You may not be able to fill all the gaps. Use your dictionary for help.

adjective	noun	adverb	verb
	children		
			encourage
			develop
	comprehension		
	advertisement		
	product		
			decide
aware			

10 In the box there are 12 words taken from the text in this workbook. Match each word with its antonym in the list below.

| negative   fully   persuasive   wider   informed   direct |
| substantial   major   general   youngest   restrict   useful |

positive
partially
minor
oldest
useless
dissuasive
narrower
misinformed
indirect
small
specific
broaden

11 Choose **eight** words from Exercise 10 and use them to write meaningful sentences.

Example:
Her school report was very <u>positive</u> about her improvement in English.

Vocabulary box

advert

Comes from the French word 'avertir' which means 'to warn'. This was originally a Latin word, 'advertere' meaning 'to turn towards'. Commercial messages (advertisements) have been found from as far back as the time of Pompeii, Italy (nearly 2,000 years ago!).

5

In this unit you will have more opportunity to do some examination practice with exam practice questions which focus on the exercises covered in the coursebook (reading & writing 1, 2 & 6, and listening).

Exam Exercise 2 (core question)

Read the newspaper article and then answer the questions which follow.

Computer games health hazards

Doctors are becoming increasingly concerned about the health of children who spend hour after hour glued to computer games. The experts say that young people are exposing themselves to a range of potential hazards, from 'mouse elbow' to 'joystick digit'.

As many as twenty per cent of children have some kind of health problem associated with the overuse of computer games, a recent survey has shown. One in seven children spend so much time in front of video screens that they have black rings around their eyes because of lack of sleep, say the doctors, who interviewed over 1,100 six to eleven year olds and their parents. One in five children showed evidence of stiff muscles in their back and shoulders, a result of the strain from the constant use of a computer mouse or video game joystick.

This study is the most recent in a series of reports which link health problems with excessive use of video and computer games. All the problems result from repetitive movements and sleep deprivation, and some experts predict that overuse of games could cause long-term heart damage.

'Mouse elbow' is the result of damage to the forearm and elbow. The elbow can also suffer trauma injury if the mouse is moved too vigorously. 'Video eyes' are caused by too little sleep. 'Joystick digit' is a consequence of overuse of the finger on the joystick. 'Vibration finger' is caused by excessive use of computer game controllers which vibrate. 'Nerve trap' is the result of the neck and head being in the same position for too long.

a What has caused doctors to become concerned about the health of children? [1]
b What percentage of children have a health problem, according to the survey? [1]
c Why do one in seven children have black rings around their eyes? [1]
d How many children and parents were interviewed for the research? [1]
e How old were the children who were interviewed? [1]
f What **two** things do doctors say that the health problems result from? [2]
g How could the heart be damaged? [1]
h List the **five** specific problems identified in the research. [2]

[Total: 10]

Exam Exercise 6 (core and extended question)

> ### 'Save our playing field' campaign!
>
> The playing field next to our school is the only place nearby where we can play sports. In the summer, the field is also used for festivals, and the popular 'world music' concert. Now it is be sold to a developer so that a new shopping centre can be built! Don't let this happen! Write to your local newspaper expressing your opinions about the importance of the playing field.
>
> Find out more: www.noshops.com

You have read the above announcement on posters in your town. Write a letter to your friend:

– giving reasons why the playing field should be saved
– saying why your community needs the playing field
– giving alternative suggestions for the site of the new shopping centre.

Your letter should be about 100–150 (core) / 150–200 (extended) words long.

Exam Exercise 1 (extended question)

Read the newsletter below. Then answer the questions which follow.

> ### Welcome!
>
> Welcome to the new Achileas sports centre and swimming pool complex monthly newsletter! We offer a wide variety of activities for you and all your family and friends. Whether your interest is fitness, football, tennis, basketball or swimming, we can offer you an excellent range of activities to suit all your needs. We hope you will enjoy your visit to the new Achileas complex and take advantage of the many facilities available.
>
> **Opening hours**
>
> *Swimming Pool*
> Monday – Friday   07.00 – 22.00
> Saturday – Sunday & Public Holidays   08.00 – 21.00
>
> *Sports Centre*
> Monday – Friday   06.00 – 22.00
> Saturday – Sunday & Public Holidays   09.00 – 20.00
>
> *Achileas Restaurant*
> Monday – Saturday   12.00 – 15.00 & 19.00 – 23.00
> Sunday & Public Holidays   12.00 – 15.00 only

Membership

	Children (6–18)	Adults (18+)	Partners (2 adults)	Family (2 adults + children)
Annual	£100	£200	£150 each	£450
6-monthly	£70	£120	£105 each	£255
3-monthly	£50	£75	£65 each	£195
Monthly	£25	£45	£40 each	£120
Weekly	£15	£35	£30 each	£90
Daily	£4	£8	£6	£14

Facilities

4 fitness & special focus gyms, 1 children's gym, Olympic pool and children's starter pool, 4 squash courts, 4 badminton courts, 2 basketball courts, 8 outdoor tennis courts, 2 all-weather football pitches, Achileas Sports Shop, Achileas Restaurant

Focus on gyms

Whatever your fitness level, whatever your age and whatever your goals, we have something to offer you in one of our special focus gyms! If you would like to lose weight, tone up, increase your strength or improve your health, we have highly qualified staff on hand to motivate you in one of our 'focus' gyms.

Whether you wish to work out once a week or every day for ten minutes or an hour, after an initial consultation, our staff will design your own personal fitness programme, tailored to suit your individual needs. You will also benefit from regular reviews, where your progress will be monitored and your programme updated or adjusted accordingly.

All of this takes place in one of our 4 focus gyms: cardiovascular, resistance training, free weights, general and sports injury.

All of our focus gyms offer state-of-the-art machines and excellent user-friendly equipment, catering for all your health and fitness needs.

a What time does the sports centre close on public holidays? [1]
b What is the cost for a family for a 6-month membership? [1]
c How many swimming pools are there? [1]
d What non-sport facility does the complex offer? [1]
e What do you need to do before the staff can design your personal fitness programme? [1]
f How is your progress assessed? [1]
g What **two** things do all of the 'focus' gyms offer? [2]

[Total: 8]

Listening exercise

Track 2

Listen to the following interview about dangers in the home, and then complete the notes below.

You will hear the interview twice.

Dangers in the home

a Safety is perhaps the most important …… that young children need to learn [1]
b Most accidents occur in the living room, bedroom, kitchen and …… [1]
c …… account for the greatest number. [1]
d Medicines should be …… and out of reach. [1]
e Dangers of electricity:
   – overloading powerpoints
   – not checking …… [1]
f …… cause a lot of accidents [1]
g Children must learn that …… and …… are not toys. [1]
h Two other dangers in the home:
   – …… and …… [1]
i After 30 minutes a hot drink can still …… [1]

[Total: 9]

Unit 6

Task 1

1 You are going to read a text about parents educating their children at home instead of sending them to school. Before you look at the text, read these questions and make some notes.

   a What do you think the benefits of being educated at home might be? Think about parents as well as children.
   b What different experiences do you think a child might have learning away from a school environment?

2 Before you write a summary, you first need to find the key points in a passage. This exercise will help you. Read the passage *I want to educate my children at home*. Then look at the sentences below and decide which ones are true, based on what you have read.

   a Parents are natural teachers from their child's birth.
   b Children need their parents to teach them.
   c School improves the natural ability of the child to learn.
   d Schools have only existed since recent times.
   e Schools become a negative struggle for many children.
   f Home schooling has proven to be beneficial to the child's academic standards.
   g Socialisation is achieved by putting children into organised groups.
   h Children who choose their own groups to mix in grow into confident adults.

I want to educate my children at home

From the day your child was born you have been home educating – assisting them in their quest for knowledge of the world around them, answering their questions, teaching them to walk and talk. You have already done the hard stuff, and without a curriculum. In fact, if you truthfully look back at this stage, you yourself have not had much of a hand in all the wonderful things your child has accomplished. Our children are born with the ability to teach themselves everything they need to know about surviving in the world they live in, and they do it well. School interrupts this natural flow of learning and eventually kills it. If you leave children alone and just provide lots of resources, encouragement and a caring environment, that is all you will ever need. Trust them and they will get the job done.

Home school is an option open to families in Australia and often the decision to home educate your child is made well after your child has started school. Schools are a fairly recent invention of man as they have only been around for about 150 years or so. Before that, parents always taught their children at home, and it was a natural part of life. Going to school is not the natural way for a child to learn and many children struggle with the concept of school. As a result, parents often see a change for the worse in their children. They become unhappy, angry little people unable to communicate with parents and siblings as they once did.

An Australian lecturer in education, who has been researching home education for ten years, has found that children who have had structured lessons at home as well as children who have had absolutely no structure at home have both turned out to be socially and academically ahead of schooled peers. The only drawback that he found in the ten years of study was the lost wages of one parent.

Children do not need to be placed in artificial situations so that they can 'become socialised'. Socialisation forced upon children in schools and playgroups is not true socialisation. Real socialisation happens all the time, every minute of the day with parents, siblings, shopkeepers, in the park and best of all, children with themselves and their dreams. It happens all the time and we do not need to set it up. The type of socialisation that does happen in the schoolyard is not the type most of us want for our children (the bullying and the peer pressure and the bad language) and children that grow up in charge of their own socialisation grow strong and confident and able to communicate with a wide range of people.

Adapted from 'I have made the decision to home educate my children'
www.home-ed.vic.edu.au/About/Decided.htm 09/02/2004

3 Write out the sentences from Exercise 2 which you think are correct.

4 Answer these questions.

  a Who plays a more important role in a child's development, according to the writer?
  b Why does the writer think that schools interrupt the 'natural flow of learning'?
  c When do parents usually start to think about home schooling for their children?
  d What sort of 'little people' are schools seen to produce?
  e What does the writer say are the benefits of home schooling?
  f What negative socialising does a school have on a child?

Task 2

5 The following words and phrases appear in the text you are going to read. Match them to the correct definition. Use your dictionary for help.

| contribute   short   salary   graduate   academic   reputation |
| initially   depend   expenses |

a connected to education   **d** costs   **g** good name
b money you earn   **e** to begin with   **h** person who has a university degree
c not enough   **f** to add   **i** rely

6 Find the vocabulary from Exercise 5 in the text.

7 The title of the following text is *I was concerned I would be left out*. What do you think the speaker meant by 'left out' here? Tick **a**, **b** or **c**.

  a left out = on my own
  b left out = left alone
  c left out = not included in a group

8 Skim the text and check if your answer to question 7 is correct.

I was concerned I would be left out

Emilia always knew that she wanted to go to university when she got her IGCSE results. But she had been worried that she would not be accepted by the other students once she got there. Although she had always been told at her school that she would do well at university, she nonetheless believed that other students would be better than her. 'I know I got good grades at school, but I thought that wouldn't be enough and that I would be left out by the other students,' she admits. Some of her friends thought she shouldn't even think about going to university but she didn't agree with that and said, 'I think university should be for everyone, no matter where they come from or what their background is.'

Growing up in a large family, she'd always understood that her parents would depend on the children to contribute money to the home. 'We all knew we'd have to help pay the expenses at home, so when I told my parents I wanted to do my IGCSEs before going to university, they weren't very pleased initially,' she recalls. 'But soon they accepted the idea when they thought about the advantages of having a university graduate in the family.'

Money was short at home, so Emilia worked after her IGCSEs and saved nearly everything from her salary. She wanted to work in medicine so she looked around and found a university near home, which meant she could stay at home and study at the same time.

The university had a good academic reputation and she thought she wouldn't get in, so she was very excited when she was offered a place. 'I never thought it possible,' she admits.

Three years later and she remembers her fears of being left out. 'I've made some really great friends and everybody has been so helpful, even the lecturers!' The idea that you are not good enough because you are different is so wrong – university is not like that.

She wants to say to other families, 'If your child is good enough and really wants to go on to university then you can't imagine the advantages there will be for you and your family.'

9 Complete these sentences based on the text.

a When Emilia got her IGCSE results …
b Although she had been told she'd do well at university …
c Emilia thinks that university is for …
d Emilia's parents expected her to …
e Emilia worked …
f The university had …
g She needn't have been afraid …
h She wants to tell other families …

10 Imagine you are someone who was educated the 'homeschool' way. You now want to go to university as Emilia did. What do you think would be your strengths and weaknesses at university? Use the table below to make notes.

	strengths	weaknesses
Socialising		
Applying yourself to a structured education		
Dealing with external deadlines and pressures		
Style of work demanded by the university		
Other points		

Language focus

11 These words appear in the text in Exercise 2. What are their opposites? Use your dictionary for help.

born – died	recent
answering – questioning	worse
teaching	artificial
hard	strong
wonderful	confident
often	wide

12 These words have been taken from unit 6, but the letters have been jumbled up. Write them out correctly. Use your dictionary to check your spelling. The first letter has been given.

Examples:
i i a y b l t = **ability**
n e i o t d u a c = **education**

s i t u e v y i r n – **u** _____   g s b s i i n l – **s** _____

s p e u r e s r – **p** _____   p c n e t c o – **c** _____

r t i t p r n e u – **i** _____   y s a t b u e o l l – **a** _____

y s l o d r c o h a – **s** _____   t n u a e e o g e c r m n – **e** _____

d r u s c e t u t r – **s** _____   s s s i i g n a t – **a** _____

13 Now match the words in Exercise 12 to the correct definition below.

  a brothers and sisters
  b completely
  c a place for advanced learning
  d helping
  e idea
  f a place of play
  g support
  h to be a part of something
  i to stop someone or something
  j demands

14 In the two texts there are some examples of phrasal verbs.

Examples:
look back – remember
depend on – trust

Match these other phrasal verbs to the correct meaning. Use your dictionary for help.

get off	extinguish
go in for	take part in something
go for	test
point out	get little punishment
try out	call attention to
put out	try to get something

15 Write **six** sentences of your own using the phrasal verbs from Exercise 14.

Vocabulary box

ostracise

The ancient Greeks held elections to decide if someone was an undesirable citizen. Votes were written on pieces of broken pottery (ostrakon). People voted undesirable were sent away, or ostracised.

Unit 6   33

Unit 7

In unit 7 of the coursebook you reviewed the skills required for note-making. Some of them were:

- Read the instructions very carefully.
- Do not write complete sentences – write notes!
- Sometimes you may only need to write a few words for each of your answers.
- Each bullet mark requires you to write something.
- Use your own words as far as possible.

Task 1

1 Skim the *Have a nice mouth* text. Match each paragraph with a subject from the list below.

   a bad breath
   b vitamin C foods
   c gum disease
   d gum inflammation
   e smoking
   f Xylitol sweetener

2 Find these words in the text. What do you think they mean? Use your dictionary for help.

   a oral (paragraph 1)
   b decay (1)
   c rinses (2)
   d hailed (2)
   e suppresses (2)
   f inhibits (2)
   g inflammation (3)
   h susceptible (3)
   i heal (3)
   j misconceptions (4)
   k advocates (4)
   l constricting (5)

3 Look at the text again. Pick out what you think are the important pieces of information in each paragraph.

Task 2

4 Read the article about gums and teeth, and complete the task which follows it.

Have a nice mouth

(1) Periodontal, or gum, disease affects 95 per cent of people, making it the most common of all diseases. It is also the leading cause of tooth loss in adults. Most people are aware of the basics of dental and oral health: twice-daily toothbrushing and regular flossing, dental checks and visits to the hygienist are essential, along with a low sugar intake. But there are other easy steps to reduce the risk of tooth decay, bleeding gums and bad breath.

(2) Plaque builds up as a mixture of mouth bacteria and food particles in a solution of mucus. A sweetener, Xylitol, which is finding its way into many chewing gums, mouth rinses and toothpastes, is being hailed as the latest effective anti-plaque weapon. Dr Ronnie Levine of the Health Development Agency says: 'As an anti-plaque and anti-caries (tooth decay) agent, Xylitol is possibly the most promising development since the introduction of fluoride.' Xylitol is a bulk sweetener, related to sugar and extracted from birch wood. Unlike most other sugars, Xylitol cannot be converted to acid in the mouth by bacteria. It suppresses unfavourable mouth bacteria, and inhibits plaque formation. A recent study showed that the children of mothers who regularly chewed Xylitol-sweetened gum had a 70 per cent reduction in tooth decay. Sugar-free gums are also a good way of encouraging saliva flow for those who suffer from xerostomia, or dry mouth.

(3) The first sign of periodontal disease is inflammation of the gums, or gingivitis, which develops in pockets between the gum and bone as it progresses. One natural compound showing promise in dealing with this is hyaluronic acid, which is found naturally in the gum and the eye. It has been used to treat eyes after surgery; now it is being used for gum health. Research is in its early stages, but Dr Peter Galgut, a specialist in periodontics, has been using it for about 18 months to control pockets of inflammation. 'It gives significant advantage for promoting healing of gingival pockets in susceptible people, as well as helping to heal mouth ulcers and a type of oral eczema,' he says.

(4) Halitosis (bad breath) plagues many people. Dr Phil Stemmer, founder of the Fresh Breath Centre, says there are two main misconceptions about bad breath: 'The first is that it comes from the stomach, which is physically impossible unless there is a damaged sphincter at the top of the stomach. The other is that a major cause is sulphurous gases given off by oral bacteria.' After brushing and flossing, Dr Stemmer advocates using a tongue scraper, which gets rid of food debris coating the tongue and reduces the reserve of bacteria in the mouth. Another unexpected, but logical, suggestion is to brush your teeth before breakfast to get rid of the bacteria, so they are unable to react with the food to create acid. Acids form within seconds of food entering the mouth, and within a minute or two are strong enough to eat away at tooth enamel.

(5) Another hazard for oral health is smoking, which, apart from creating a risk of oral cancer, increases gum disease by constricting blood vessels that deliver nutrients to the gums, contributing to bone breakdown and slowing healing of the tissues. One study concluded that smokers had 38 per cent bone loss compared with nine per cent in non-smokers. Smokers need to take extra vitamin C for gum health, as smoking destroys this nutrient.

(6) Some nutrients are important for oral health, and bleeding gums can be an early sign of scurvy, caused by a deficiency or lack of vitamin C. Trials have shown that eating more vitamin C rich foods, such as citrus fruit, kiwi, strawberries, broccoli and cabbage, can reverse vitamin C related bleeding gums. While it may sound obvious advice, calcium has been linked in several studies to increased periodontal disease, and it is important to make sure that you get at least 700mg daily in your diet, from foods such as yoghurt, cheese, green leafy vegetables, nuts, seeds, canned sardines or salmon and bread.

Adapted from *The Times*, p. 12, Suzannah Olivier, 28/08/01

You are going to give a talk about oral hygiene to a group of students at your school. You have decided to use information from this article in your talk. To help plan your talk, make two short notes under each of the following headings:

a The basics of gum and oral health   c Causes of bad breath

b Facts about Xylitol   d Sources of vitamin C and calcium   [8]

Language focus

5 In the coursebook texts these **relative pronouns** were used:

A caterer is a person <u>who</u> is paid to provide food and drinks at a party or meeting.
The kit consists of four straps <u>which</u> attach to your trampoline and to stakes in the ground.

Now write complete sentences using the correct relative pronoun (some pronouns will have to be used more than once).

There is a film on at the cinema		people play tennis.
A fireman is a person		they got married?
Is this the article in the newspaper	who	I would like to see.
Do you know the reason	which	it was valued more than it is now.
Do you think they would forget the day	that	is a small island.
A cathedral is a place	where	passed all her exams.
That was the girl	when	talks about the best hotels?
The carpenter is from a place	why	loves his job.
Their craft is from a time		they went on strike?
Wimbledon is a club		is usually quiet and peaceful.

6 In the coursebook the words *a<u>ss</u>embling* and *profe<u>ss</u>ional* appear.

Use the table below to make more words which are spelt with *-ss-*:

a		ive
a		ue
ba		ette
pa		ertion
ca		inet
me	ss	ive
ma		port
ti		ume
succe		age
pa		ful

Example:
a<u>ss</u>ertion

7 Match the words from Exercise 6 to a definition below:

Example:
to think something is true – assume

    a paper handkerchief

    b very large

    c opposite of active

    d something you strongly believe

    e official book you must travel with

    f to think something is true

    g doing well

    h magnetic tape

    i information given to someone

    j small bed for a young baby

8 Look at the passage *An art no more?* on page 53 of your coursebook and answer the following questions.

Find **five** adjectives in the first paragraph. The first letter is given to you.

Example: *quick-moving*

    a w_____   **b** m_____   **c** t_____   **d** a_____   **e** d_____

    f In paragraph 2 find an adjective. Write down the comparative and superlative forms of that adjective.
Example: *large – larger – largest*

    g Find **four** examples of compound nouns used in the text.
Example: *saw + dust = sawdust*

    h Find synonyms for these words in the text.
Example: *assist – help*

    very
    sensitive
    wood
    special
    present

Vocabulary box

tooth

The word comes from the Old English 'toth'. It is connected to the Latin 'dens', which explains why we go to the dentist and not the tooth doctor!

Unit 8

Task 1

1 Read this exam-type question.

> Your teacher is planning a special weekend trip for you and your classmates. During the weekend you will be able to take part in various activities that you do not normally do at school.
>
> Your teacher wants your ideas for what activities might be offered. S/he has suggested soccer, tennis, kickboxing and karate.
>
> Write a letter to your teacher about the activities you would like to take part in. You can choose from your teacher's ideas, or make your own suggestions.
>
> In your letter say:
> – what the activity involves
> – why you want to do it
> – why it would be suitable for other members of your class.
>
> **Your letter should be about 150–200 words long.**

2 In this particular question, there is quite a lot of information for you to read and understand. Do the following:

a Read the question very carefully.
b Put all the words which give you general information in one list.
c Put all the words which give you instructions in a second list.
d Put all the words which tell you what you have to write about in a third list.

To answer this question, you need to:

- write a letter to your teacher
- describe the activity you want to do
- tell him/her why you want to do it
- explain why your friends would enjoy the activity.

Task 2

3 Read the sample answer below and complete the gaps with suitable words or phrases from the box.

> I hope that you will …   I like the idea of …   I think having …   I'd like to play …
> I'm writing to let you know …   I've never done …   My idea is to …
> we could have…   we never have much chance to …

Dear Mr Pilot

(1) … which activity I would like to do during our special weekend school trip.

(2) … kickboxing before, but as I am afraid of being hurt, I don't think that would be a good activity for me to do! (3) … soccer, but I think that at this time of the year it will be too hot with all that running about. (4) … tennis, but I did that last year with my family.

(5) … take our bikes with us and to go for a long ride. At the end of the ride (6) … a barbecue or a picnic. Everyone in our class has a suitable bike and here in the town (7) … ride in the countryside, so I think this would be a wonderful opportunity for all of us. Also, (8) … a barbecue or picnic when we finish would make us all ride very fast!

(9) … consider my suggestion – I can't wait for our weekend trip!

Best wishes

Alex
(190 words)

4 Answer this exam practice question:

> You recently went on a weekend activity trip with your classmates. During the weekend you took part in activities that you do not normally do at school.
>
> Write an article for your school or college magazine in which you describe what activities you took part in.
>
> In your article you should include the following:
>
> – where you went and what activities you did
> – what you thought of the activity weekend
> – whether or not you would recommend the activity weekend
>
> **Your article should be about 150–200 words long.**

Language focus

5 Here are some commonly used British English (BrE) and American English (AmE) words. Complete the gaps. Use your dictionary for help.

	Br E	AmE
Example:	colour	color
	analyse	_____
	travelled	_____
	programme	_____
	cheque	_____
	_____	labor
	_____	theater
	_____	donut
	centre	_____
	metre	_____
	gaol	_____
	_____	humor
	_____	pajamas
	honour	_____
	_____	catalog
	_____	maneuver
	_____	tire
	practise (v) practice (n)	_____
	aeroplane	_____

6 There are 10 words in the wordsearch box which have something to do with letter writing, or which you may write in a letter. How many can you find?

F	S	I	G	N	A	T	U	R	E
A	F	X	A	D	D	R	E	S	S
I	O	Y	D	E	A	R	W	X	X
T	R	I	N	F	O	R	M	A	L
H	M	Z	D	L	T	E	Y	L	B
F	A	T	A	H	X	P	O	F	K
U	L	N	T	Q	T	L	U	H	T
L	T	W	E	P	P	Y	R	K	M
L	Z	Y	X	Q	B	Y	S	M	L
Y	S	I	N	C	E	R	E	L	Y

7 In your coursebook you will find these words.

Internet – a computer system used to exchange information worldwide
electronic language – specially adapted language to use on electronic equipment

Here are more words. Some are rather strange. Match each one to its correct definition.

buzzy	press the button on a computer mouse
click	a computer file appended to an email
tweenager	a middle-aged person associated with youth culture
retail therapy	lively and exciting
attachment	loose-fitting cotton trousers with large pockets
digital divide	to determine the size, shape and form of a written document
mobe	division between those who have and those who don't have computers
adultescent	mobile phone
to format	a child between the ages of 10 and 14
cargo pants	the practice of shopping to make you feel happy

8 Complete the gaps in the following sentences using a suitable word from Exercise 7.

 a The …… between rich and poor nations is becoming more obvious as technology improves.
 b She is a real……, as dolls are of no interest to her any more. She's outgrown them.
 c Unhappy people often find …… helps them improve their frame of mind, but then they are left with the bills to pay.
 d There were a lot of older people at the pop concert. They are obviously going through their …… stage of life.
 e I've received your email, but there is no …… so I haven't got the information I need.
 f The party was great. There was a really …… atmosphere all night.
 g Just call me on my …… if you need me.
 h Don't forget to left …… if you want to highlight something.
 i Remember to correctly …… all the documents before you hand in your project.
 j These …… are great and practical for travelling in.

9 Here are **five** more words. Find definitions for them and write a sentence using each word correctly.

 a browser
 b mitch
 c garage (not the car type!)
 d duvet day
 e yah (not hello!)

Vocabulary box

letter

This comes from the Latin word 'littera', which refers to letters of the alphabet.

Unit 9

Task 1

1 Here is the title of an article you are going to read:

Folk maestro looks back on life in dance

Which of the descriptions below best matches the title?

– A person who knows about different types of dance
– A famous traditional dancer who is now too old to dance
– A young dancer talks about another famous dancer

2 Scan the text and find these numbers. What do they refer to?

Example: *98 – age the ex-dancer is during the interview*

a 12
b 1906
c 1920
d 1937
e 1945
f 1955
g 1943
h 50
i 4

Folk maestro looks back on life in dance

Igor Moiseyev has refused to give up work. At the age of 98, the head of Russia's best-known folk dance group continues to go to work every day, and takes part in training dancers.

A small figure in a black cap, Moiseyev has kept the distinguished looks that helped him in his first career as a classical dancer at the Bolshoi Theatre in Moscow.

'I think I'm the only one, not just in dance, but in any area, who works at the age of 98,' says Moiseyev. 'I don't want to retire.' The artistic director both of the group and its training school spends several hours each day at work, aided by his younger wife Irini, who, like the other staff, is one of his former dancers.

'Igor Moiseyev most of all enjoys going to the young children's lessons,' said director Yelena Shcherbakova about the school, which trains dancers from the age of 12 for a possible place in the group.

Born in Kiev in 1906, Moiseyev first got interested in dance while travelling across the Ukrainian countryside with his aunts, who worked as teachers. In 1920 his father enrolled him in a dance school, hoping that dance would give him skills that a young man needs. He then moved quickly up the career ladder, but his dream was to perform folk dance professionally, and, in 1937, he formed a small company. In 1945, the company became the first Soviet dance group to travel abroad, and in 1955 toured France and Britain, where Moiseyev recalled that the group was particularly enthusiastic about watching 'Scottish dancers in kilts'.

Like the Bolshoi Theatre and other cultural organisations, Moiseyev's dance group receives finance from the government, and is just as popular today as it was in the past. 'It's enough to come to our concerts and see how many are in the audience and how they receive us,' Moiseyev says.

But there are some differences, Moiseyev admitted. Russian pop music has partly overshadowed the folk heritage. 'I think that for some reason more attention is given to pop, while I cultivated folk music,' he said.

The Moiseyev tradition is set to continue as long as the group's school, founded in 1943, keeps training new generations of dancers. Fifty pupils of both sexes graduate every four years, with the best joining the dance group.

Adapted from www.moscowtimes.ru/stories/ 21/02/2004

3 These sentences are based on the text. Decide if they are true or false.

  a Igor Moiseyev no longer goes to work every day.
  b He first became a folk dancer at the Bolshoi Theatre.
  c His wife, Irini, used to be a dancer.
  d All his dancers are guaranteed a place in his dance group.
  e His father thought that dance would be important.
  f Igor was mainly interested in folk dance.
  g He travelled abroad in 1945 to France and Britain.
  h The government gives support to his group.
  i He thinks that folk dance is as popular as pop culture.
  j Every year pupils graduate from the school.

4 Rewrite the false sentences to make them true.

  Example:
  Igor Moiseyev no longer goes to work every day.
  Igor Moiseyev continues to go to work every day.

Task 2

You are going to hear an Indian classical dancer talking about her career.

5 Before you listen, match the words and phrases taken from the text with a similar word or phrase. Do not worry about the 'tick' column at the moment.

word from text	match	tick
classical	experts	
crucial	decision	
debutante	vital	
critics	traditional	
judgement	important	
raved	poor	
prestigious	support	
choreography	reporters	
irrespective of	with no regard to	
impoverished	newcomer	
connoisseurs	enthused	
promote	dance composition	

6 Listen to the text. Tick off the words in Exercise 5 as you hear them. *Track 3*

7 Listen again and match the phrases in Columns A and B to make meaningful sentences or phrases. This will help you to understand the text. *Track 3*

A	B
a the Arangetram	of India
b a special offering	by the debutante
c the judgement	group of 60 performers
d has the unique distinction	of the critics is crucial
e to dance at the prestigious	residence of the President
f leading dance gurus	as her contribution to society
g different dance forms	children and the poor
h enjoys teaching	is the most crucial performance
i she dances	of making over 1,600 live performances
j she has her own	such as Indian folk dancing

Example:
a *The Arangetram is the most crucial performance.*

8 Read and answer the following questions. Use the tapescript to check your answers.

  a How is the performance of the 'Arangetram' important to a new dancer?
  b What response did Dr Sinduri receive when she performed the 'Arangetram'?
  c In what way was Dr Sinduri different to other dancers who had performed at the President's residence?
  d Name **four** things that Mr Pillai's style of teaching includes.
  e Who does Dr Sinduri particularly enjoy teaching?
  f Name **one** social problem in India which Dr Sinduri mentions.
  g How long was her solo performance?
  h Name **five** countries she has visited.

Language focus

9 Look at these sentences from the text about Igor Moiseyev.

Igor Moiseyev <u>has refused</u> to give up work. At the age of 98, the head of Russia's best-known folk dance group <u>continues</u> to go to work every day, and <u>takes</u> part in training dancers.

A small figure in a black cap, Moiseyev <u>has kept</u> the distinguished looks that <u>helped</u> him in his first career as a classical dancer at the Bolshoi Theatre in Moscow.

Match the underlined verbs with the correct tense from the box:

present   present perfect   past

When we write about the experiences of a living person, we often need to use these three tenses in order to:

describe what the person did in the past (e.g. finished events) – PAST
describe what the person has done during their life (e.g. experiences) – PRESENT PERFECT
describe what the person does now (e.g. habits) – PRESENT

10 Read the text again. Find as many verbs as you can which occur in the past, present perfect or present tense. For each verb, make sure you identify when the event occurred or occurs.

11 Think about your own life so far. Write a short paragraph (about 100 words) in which you describe what you did in the past (e.g. finished events), things you have done during your life (e.g. experiences) and what you do now (e.g. habits).

12 Dr Sinduri says: *I love to teach dance to all those interested, <u>irrespective of</u> their age and ability. Irrespective of* here means that 'age and ability' are of no importance.

Use the following pieces of information to write complete sentences using *irrespective of*. You will need to think carefully about what you write.

Example:
repair the damage / cost not important
We will repair the damage irrespective of the cost.

    a win the race / tiredness not important
    b complete the puzzle / difficulty not important
    c go for a walk / weather not important
    d go swimming / temperature of water not important
    e visit China / language not a problem

13 Complete the word puzzle by adding these words to the word **choreograph**.

artistic	critics	group	theatre
classical	dance	performance	training
concert	folk	technique	

C H O R E O G R A P H

Vocabulary box

dance

The word dates back to the 13th century and comes from the Old English 'daunces' and originally from the Old French 'danser'. The actual origin is uncertain.

Unit 10

In this unit you will be able to do some examination practice with exam practice questions which focus on the exercises covered in the coursebook (reading & writing 2, 3 & 7, and listening).

Exam Exercise 2 (core question)

The value of cheese ...

Parmesan cheese, without which your plate of spaghetti just does not taste right, has for many years been used as security for loans by banks in the north of Italy. In a vast warehouse near the town of Parma, owned by the Banco Credito Emiliano, there are literally hundreds of thousands of wheels of cheese, each one ripening by the day, and increasing in value as they mature.

The cheeses offer short-term financing for local people until the cheese is ready to sell. Most banks will provide loans of between 65% and 70% of the value of the cheese when it enters the warehouse. A fresh wheel of parmesan usually weighs about 50 kg, but as it matures it will lose about 20% (or 10 kg) of its initial weight. However, the more mature a cheese becomes, the greater its value.

After the first 12 months in the warehouse, parmesan cheese is worth about $10.50 per kilo, whereas after two years the price has more than doubled. In some large London stores, two-year-old parmesan sells to the public for $45 per kilo.

For the banks around Parma, parmesan cheese has offered a very low security risk for more than 70 years. The process itself is painstaking, and dates back to the 14th century when Benedictine monks first made the now world-famous cheese. While the machinery as well as the financing has changed over the years, the love and care which goes into the production of parmesan cheese remains unique. Rows of large copper containers, called vats, steam as warm milk bubbles and froths; the cheese mixture is whipped, heated, and then cooled; finally the soft cheese is placed in a net-like bag, and then into a mould.

But modern technology now provides each wheel of parmesan with its own personal air-conditioning system, which ensures that the air surrounding it is cooled to 18–20 degrees centigrade, with an air humidity level of 80%. There is even a special room where cheeses which have suffered some type of superficial damage can receive special attention.

Read the article above and then answer the questions which follow.

    a What happens to the value of a wheel of parmesan as it ripens? [1]
    b How much does a full-size parmesan weigh once it has matured? [1]
    c Who were the first people to make parmesan cheese? [1]
    d What happens to the cheese mixture after it has cooled? [1]
    e What has been the effect of modern technology on the parmesan cheese making process? [2]
    f Make a list of **four** pieces of information about the financial value of parmesan cheese. [4]
    [Total: 10]

Exam Exercise 3 (extended question)

You attend the Instituto Acapulco, 6 San Miguel de Allende, 1022 Mexico City. Your school's headteacher has informed you that your class will be attending a humanities course in Belize. Your geography teacher at the school has asked you to research all the information and to complete the application form for your class.

Information

A total of 28 students (16 girls and 12 boys) will attend the course, accompanied by 3 teachers. The students will be accommodated in pairs at the course centre. The course itself will last for 5 days, from Monday 20 June until Friday 24 June. However, because of the long journey, the group will depart from Mexico City on the Saturday before the start of the course, and return on Saturday 25 June. Meals will be served during the course as follows: breakfast at 0800, lunch at 1300 and dinner at 1900. The course starts at 0900 and finishes at 1700 each day.

The course centre has full leisure facilities for your group to relax. Wednesday 22 June will be a half-day, and during the afternoon there will be an organised programme of activities. In your group, nearly everyone enjoys swimming and tennis; some students enjoy sightseeing and shopping; others enjoy quiet indoor activities and games. The swimming pool is only open at the weekend, but the tennis courts are open every day. There is a free bus which can be pre-booked for visits away from the course centre. You will need the bus to transport everyone from and to the airport.

Three people in your group are vegans, and one girl is partially sighted and will need the course materials in large print.

As you are studying IGCSE South American geography, it would be very helpful if the course organisers were aware of this in order to plan the most useful course sessions for you.

COURSE APPLICATION FORM

Name of your organisation: _____

Address: _____

Course required: _____

Total number of people: _____

Duration of stay:

From: _____   To: _____

Student accommodation:

Male rooms: _____   Female rooms: _____

Activities for group (please tick):

☐ Swimming   ☐ Basketball   ☐ Sightseeing   ☐ Indoor games

Suggestions for other activities:

Meal times:
Please delete times NOT required

Breakfast   0700   0800
Lunch   1200   1300
Dinner   1900   2000

Special requests:

a _____

b _____

c _____

Write a paragraph of about 60 words to briefly describe what type of programme would be most beneficial to your group

Exam Exercise 7 (core and extended question)

You recently attended a sports event at the new stadium in your home town. Write a letter to the manager of the stadium explaining why you were dissatisfied with the sports event and the new facilities, and asking for your money to be refunded.

Your letter should be 100–150 (core) / 150–200 (extended) words long.

Listening exercise   Track 4

Listen to the following interview about a mathematical discovery, and then answer the questions below. You will hear the interview twice.

a	Why are prime numbers so important?	[1]
b	How many digits does the recently discovered prime number have?	[1]
c	Why might it be a waste of time to try to find a prime number?	[1]
d	What was the $50,000 prize awarded for?	[1]
e	How long did it take Michael Cameron's computer to find the prime?	[1]
f	What made Mr Cameron decide to start the search for a prime?	[1]
g	How many prime numbers are there?	[1]

[Total: 7]

Unit 11

Task 1

1 Skim the four short texts below and decide which of the job titles in the box fits each one. What helps you to decide?

forest fire fighter	steeplejack	goldminer	deep sea diver

> **A** Numerous North Sea diving deaths in the 1970s and 1980s prompted a safety drive that slashed mortality rates. But divers still face perils as they work, sometimes in total darkness, hundreds of feet down in the oceans. Hazards of the job include the bends and jellyfish stings.
>
> **B** The depths at which miners work – often more than two miles below the surface – mean that the effects of even minor earth tremors can be devastating, causing tunnels to collapse. In South Africa, where tremors are frequent, 4 men died and 11 others were trapped for days when hundreds of tons of rocks collapsed at the Orkney shaft, 100 miles south-west of Johannesburg, last year.
>
> **C** Risk of accidental death is believed to be around one in 1,000 each year. In June last year, a man died after plunging 120 feet from the roof of Edinburgh Castle.
>
> **D** In the United States, 136 pilots have lost their lives in the past 50 years as they attempted to douse flames with water. Smokejumpers, who parachute in, are even more vulnerable.

2 Vocabulary

  a Find two words in text A which have a similar meaning to 'dangers'.
  b What does 'slashed' mean in text A: 'reduced' or 'increased'?
  c Which word in text B is similar in meaning to 'vibrations'?
  d Give another word for 'plunging' in text C.
  e Guess the meaning of 'douse' in text D.

Task 2

3 You are going to read a longer text: *It's the coldest, most isolated continent on earth. Why would anyone want to work there?* What do you think the text is about?

4 These words and phrases have been removed from the text. Use your dictionary to help you find out what they mean.

auroral	motives
devoted	reigns
insomnia	swell
maintain	tang

5 Here are the meanings of the words in Exercise 4. Match each one with the correct word. Are your meanings from Exercise 4 the same?

at the start of the day
dedicated
exists
flavour
increase
look after
reasons
sleeplessness

6 Read the text and complete the gaps with the words from Exercise 4.

It's the coldest, most isolated continent on earth. Why would anyone want to work there?

Applications from steel erectors in response to an advert placed by the British Antarctic Survey to work in Antarctica are pouring in. The BAS is looking for workers to …… its southern-most research centre, the Halley base, during the continent's four-month summer.

Antarctica is the coldest and windiest continent on earth, and the Halley base is the remotest of the five British stations there. Each year 15 staff see out the long winter, when temperatures fall as low as –55 °C and darkness …… for 105 days, relieved only by the spectacular …… displays.

Even in summer, when numbers on the base …… to 65, temperatures can plummet to –28 °C. Many staff develop chronic polar …… because of the 24-hour daylight.

Everybody longs for fresh fruit and vegetables, since food supplies arrive just twice a year and must be dragged 12 km from the coast. One former staff member recalls his colleagues fantasising endlessly about the …… of tomatoes.

And people need to be sure that they can get on with the rest of the team: the nearest neighbours are 30km away and rather short on conversation, being Emperor penguins.

The Halley site, on the Brunt Ice Shelf, has been occupied by the British since 1956, but the first four bases had to be abandoned because they were crushed by ice.

The steel erectors will have to save the current set of buildings by jacking up the steel legs supporting the steel platforms, to keep them clear of the snowfall. They will also put up new masts and other structures to assist with research.

The centre is best known for its work in monitoring the hole in the ozone layer, but it also studies atmospheric pollution, sea level rise, climate change and geology.

But while scientists have often …… their lives to examining particular phenomena, support staff on the bases have other …… . Many find that a four-month contract is an ideal way to save money: pay begins at £15,000 a year, all accommodation, food and clothing come free, and there is nowhere to spend money.

Adapted from the *Guardian*, Tania Branigan, 06/08/01

Job advertisement

Antarctica, the coldest, most exhilarating and isolated continent in the world, offers exceptional challenges. We rely on motivated steel / mast erectors and fabricators to maintain buildings and facilities that support vital scientific investigations in the most hostile of environments. Shifts usually last for 12 hours for six and sometimes seven weeks.

No two days are the same. Life here is like nowhere else so you must be ready to enjoy all the challenges it offers.

Salary will be between £15,171 and £17,700 pa pro-rata with an Antarctic allowance of £1,903 pro-rata

7   Answer the following questions.

   a What is the weather like in Antarctica? Give **two** pieces of information.
   b What is the difference between the lowest summer and winter temperatures?
   c What happens to many people because of the 24-hour daylight in summer?
   d Why did the British have to leave the first four bases?
   e Apart from the ozone layer, what else does the Halley base study? Give **four** things.
   f List **four** points of advice you would give to someone applying for the job in Antarctica.

Language focus

8   The verbs below have been taken from unit 11 in the coursebook. Make a list of other words which can be formed from these verbs. Use your dictionary for help.

Example:
conquer > conquered, conqueror, conquest

   a determine
   b achieve
   c succeed
   d perish
   e dissuade
   f explore
   g isolate
   h climb

9   Choose a suitable word from Exercise 8 to complete the sentences. It could be a verb, or a word which has been formed from the verb.

Example:
The lands of the <u>conquered</u> empire experienced many years of civil wars.

   a The man who took over Maria's job, her … , is a person with a lot of experience.
   b Ivy is a very attractive plant, particularly when it has … over exterior walls.
   c Everyone in the class … high IGCSE grades this year.
   d This is an … case and very unusual and I don't think there will be another like it.
   e All … goods always have a sell-by date on their packet.
   f Everyone should be … from smoking as it is so unhealthy.
   g He was a famous … who died on one of his expeditions.
   h She always gets what she wants; she is a very … person.

10 In the coursebook there are many examples of comparatives and superlatives. Complete the table.

adjective	comparative	superlative
tall	taller	tallest
thin		
cheap		
good		
bad		
unhappy		
untidy		
clever		
lonely		
far		
much		
shy		

11 Use other superlatives to complete these world records.

Example:
The fastest time taken by a woman to win the World Championship triathlon is 1 hour and 50 minutes.

a The women of the Padaung tribe have the … necks in the world.
b The … person in medical history weighed 635 kg.
c The … ear hair sprouting from the outer ear was 13.2 cm.
d The … insect eats 86,000 times its own birth weight.
e The … dive measured was 483 m by an emperor penguin.
f The … animal in Australia is the rabbit, which eats crops, destroys seedlings and damages the soil with its burrows.
g The … hotel in the world is in Japan and dates back to AD 717.

12 Look at this sentence from the text about Antarctica. There are three superlatives which provide a detailed description:
Antarctica is the <u>coldest</u> and <u>windiest</u> continent on earth, and the Halley base is the <u>remotest</u> of the five British stations there.

Write **five** sentences of your own which use a combination of superlatives to give a full description of somewhere, somebody or something.

Vocabulary box

elephant

The elephant is one of the largest mammals on land. It gets its name from its tusks, which are made of ivory. The Greek word for 'ivory' is 'elephas'.

Unit 12

Task 1

1. In the text *Babbling babies have natural rhythm*, find words which match the following definitions.

   a a quality that you have when you are born (*adjective, para 1*)
   b ideas or methods never used before (*adjective, 1*)
   c completely (*adverb, 2*)
   d clearly different from something else (*adjective, 3*)
   e without having a clear pattern (*adjective, 4*)

2. Read the text more closely and then complete the following sentences. Use your own words as far as possible. You will need to write short phrases, not single words.

   a Babbling used to be considered … but research now shows …
   b In the research, scientists examined … and discovered two things: … and …
   c The scientists say that hearing babies with signing deaf parents make a type of rhythmic movement … which is …
   d The babbling of children with deaf parents was …
   e Nursery rhymes and the way people speak to babies …

Task 2

3. Use the notes you made in Exercise 2 to help you to answer the following question:

   Read the following article, which is about babies and their ability to use a type of sign language with their hands. Write a summary of the results of the research carried out by scientists. You should write about 100 words. Write in your own words as far as possible.

Babbling babies have natural rhythm

(1) Babies are born with an innate sense of rhythm that is essential for learning a language, according to a pioneering study of children who learnt 'silent babbling' using sign language. Babbling is common to all babies and was once thought to be merely the result of children learning to move their jaws. But research on the children of deaf parents indicates that a baby babbles to develop its inborn rhythm, which is critical for learning a language. The findings could help children with speech difficulties by providing a better understanding of how infants normally use patterns in the brain's language centres.

(2) Scientists studied the normal, hearing babies of profoundly deaf parents and found that, in addition to the random hand movements made by all babies, the infants demonstrated 'silent babbling' using rudimentary signs. By fixing lights to the tips of babies' fingers and analysing their motion, researchers identified non-random movements within normal movements.

(3) The scientists, led by Professor Laura Ann Petitto of Dartmouth College, New Hampshire, and McGill University, Montreal, write in *Nature*: 'Hearing babies with signing deaf parents make a

special kind of movement with their hands, with a specific rhythmic pattern that is distinct from the other hand movements. We figured out that this kind of rhythmic movement was linguistic … It was babbling, but with their hands.'

(4) The scientists compared three babies with normal hearing whose parents were profoundly deaf – and who therefore had little exposure to speech – with three babies born to hearing couples who talked to their children. The 'silent babbling' seen in children of deaf parents was a lower, more rhythmic activity performed closer to the body than the ordinary, random hand movements of infants. Professor Petitto said: 'This dramatic distinction between the two types of hand movements indicates that babies … can make use of the rhythmic patterns underlying human language.' The singsong way many people speak to babies and the patterns of speech in nursery rhymes could be used more effectively in helping handicapped children to speak earlier, the scientists said.

Adapted from *The Independent*, p.6, Steve Connor, 06/12/01

Language focus

4 Look at these phrases taken from the text about Vanessa Mae on page 90 of your coursebook:

… as a bonus, a video <u>montage</u> set to …
… now also lists singing in her <u>repertoire</u>, having added …

The underlined words have been 'borrowed' from the French language. Many words which are commonly used in English have come from other languages.

In the following sentences (a) find the 'borrowed' word and (b) guess which language English has borrowed it from (choose from the languages in the box).

| French   German   Hindi   Inuit (Eskimo) |

a A chameleon safely camouflages itself by adapting its skin to the background.
b The husky dog is well suited to an extremely cold environment.
c Quartz watches are normally very expensive but of excellent quality.
d Children often go to a kindergarten before they start school.
e The thugs were soon picked up by the police.
f The bride's sari was made from gorgeous silk.
g Even today the waltz is one of the most popular ballroom dances.
h The chauffeur brought the car round to the front of the hotel.
i The soldier planned to work his way up the ranks from lieutenant.
j They agreed that the best place to rendezvous would be the park.
k We normally buy some pretzels and have them for breakfast.
l An igloo does not look like a very cosy place to live.

5 Guess the meaning of the words from Exercise 4 according to their context in the sentences. Use your dictionary for help.

word	guessed meaning	dictionary definition
montage	scene	an art form with parts pieced together to form one
repertoire	list of activities	all the plays, pieces of music, etc, which a performer performs
a		
b		
c		
d		
e		
f		
g		
h		
i		
j		
k		
l		

6 Look at these other 'borrowed' words. What do they mean? Use your dictionary for help. Use each word in a sentence of your own.

a tycoon
b chimpanzee
c sleazy
d sable
e cocoa
f cosmonaut

Vocabulary box

khaki

Khaki comes from the Urdu for 'dusty'. The colour was first used on British army uniforms in India in 1846. Olive green was later added during the First World War to be used against muddy ground and trees and plants.

Unit 13

Task 1

1 Read this exam practice question and the sample answers written by two students.

> Write an article for your school or college magazine about what you think is the most important piece of equipment in your life today.  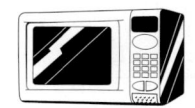  
>
> The pictures above may give you some ideas, but you are free to choose something different.
>
> In your article you should include the following:
>
> – the name of the piece of equipment, and what it does
> – what its benefit is to you
> – your reasons for choosing it
>
> **Your article should be about 150–200 words long.**

Student A

I think spaceship is one of the most important pieces of equipment for me. It offeres very quick transporting to space. Before peoples used to travel by animals and planes but nowdays they don't. It benefits to me because it means that I can go to the moon and mars and see other planets a very long distance from here. I can get there in a very quick time – much more quickly than on a horse or a donkey. They are quite safe but sometimes there are accidents and people use to die. It costs a lot of money to go to the moon and I don't think I will be able ever to pay a ticket but I really want to go one day until I die.
(128 words)

Student B

Have you ever concidered what your life would be like without all those things which make it so comfortable and easy? Yes, I'm talking about your mobil phone, camcorder, microwave oven, CD walkman, PS2, DVD player, and even youre coffee frappe whisker!

If you could keep only one thing, wich one would it be? Well, for me, there's no question that I would have to keep my mobil phone becouse it's more than just a way to call people, isn't it? You can send messiges, use your phone as a diary, keep notes in it, and of course play games! Without my mobil, nowadays I would be completly lost.

Whatever did we do before we had mobils? Did we really use those public telephones whenever we wanted to make a call? I can hardly remember writting things in a diary, and the days of having nothing to do while waiting for a friend to turn up are gone forever now that mobils have such a great selection of games!

Without my mobil I would be lost with nothing to do.
(180 words)

Which is the better answer? Why? Make a list of the strong and weak areas in each piece of writing.

student A		student B	
weak	strong	weak	strong
no paragraphs		spelling	

2 Look at the two pieces of writing again and answer these questions for each one.

  a Is the writing enjoyable to read?
  b Is there a clear beginning and ending?
  c Are there many mistakes in grammar, punctuation and spelling?
  d Have the points in the question been answered?
  e Has the student included their own ideas?

Task 2

3 Look at your list of weak areas in the two pieces of writing. With your partner, try to improve the two answers. Do not rewrite the complete composition.

4 Answer this exam practice question:

> You have just bought a new piece of equipment, such as a mobile phone, CD Walkman or PS2. Write a letter to your English-speaking friend telling him/her about it.
>
> In your letter you should explain:
>
> – what piece of equipment you have bought, and why
> – what it can do
> – how you think your life will be different with this piece of equipment
>
> **Your letter should be about 150–200 words long.**

Language focus

5 In the text *Asia-Pacific...* on page 99 of your coursebook, the infinitive clause is used as a subject.

Examples:
To continually *build* capital ...
To support research ...
To assist in funding ...

This style is usually only used **formally**. **Informally** we can use the *-ing* form:

Examples:
*Continually build*ing *capital ...*
Supporting research ...
Assisting in funding ...

Change these sentences using the informal *-ing* form.

a To meet often is a good solution.
b To eat late is not good for the digestion.
c To go to sleep early is a healthy option.
d To assist the old is beneficial to society.
e To save money is a good investment.

6 Write sentences of your own using these verbs in both the formal and informal forms.

a prepare
b campaign
c consume
d equip
e consider

7 In the text about the Scout organisation in unit 13 of the coursebook, these descriptive words are used:

global   mixed   worthwhile   environment   orientated

Which words could be used to describe the following organisations?

World Health Organisation / United Nations / Red Cross – Red Crescent / Worldwide Fund for Nature

8 These words have been taken from unit 13. Complete the table. You might not be able to fill all the gaps.

verb	noun	adjective
establish	establishment	established
		environmental
	activity	
direct		
	objective	
	campaign	
		participatory
train		
	consumer	
investigate		
		equipped

9 Find words from the table in Exercise 8 which match with these clues.

 a This word also means 'to eat'.
 b This word means 'the aim'.
 c A football coach (not the vehicle!) is also this.
 d A policeman would do this to the traffic.
 e A policeman would do this to a crime.
 f If you have this, you are ready to play football or climb a mountain.
 g This word is made up of 6 syllables.
 h This word could also refer to a battle.
 i A live volcano normally has a lot of this.
 j This word is connected to 'ecology'.

10 Look at the words in the **noun** column in Exercise 8 for only 15 seconds. How many can you remember? Write them down. The first letter has been given to you.

a e	**e** o	**i** c
b e	**f** c	**j** i
c a	**g** p	**k** e
d d	**h** t	

Vocabulary box

scout

The word originates indirectly from the Old French word 'escouter' – to listen, which comes from the Latin 'auscultare', which is connected to the medical diagnostic procedure of listening to organs like the heart (auscultation).

Unit 14

Task 1

1 You are going to read one text about Australia and listen to another text about the Caribbean. Both texts focus on animals. What do you know about Australia and the Caribbean? Make some notes about the following and set them out in a table. You might like to use an encyclopedia or the internet for help.

   a location
   b language(s) spoken
   c animals
   d important towns
   e country / continent / group of islands

Australia	Caribbean
a	a
b	b
c	c
d	d
e	e

2 Before you read, look at these words taken from the Australia text. What do they mean? Use your dictionary for help.

   a bulky
   b immature
   c mammal
   d marsupial
   e obstacles
   f pouch
   g rear
   h survive

3 Complete the text with the words from Exercise 2.

The symbol of Australia

(1) When European explorers first saw these strange hopping animals, they asked a native Australian aborigine what they were called. He replied 'kangaroo', which means 'I don't understand'. The explorers thought this was what the animal was called. And that's how the kangaroo got its name. The kangaroo was selected as a symbol of Australia to represent the country's progress because kangaroos are always moving forwards, and never move backwards.

(2) A kangaroo is a .... It is a macropod, which means 'big foot', and there are over 47 different species. The smaller ones are usually called wallabies. The largest is the Red Kangaroo, which stands taller than a man and can weigh anything up to 85 kilos. It is the largest marsupial in the world.

(3) Kangaroos usually have one baby annually. The young kangaroo, or joey, is born at a very .... stage, when it is only about 2 cm long and weighs less than a gram. Immediately after birth it crawls up the mother's body and enters the .... The baby attaches its mouth to one of four milk teats, which then enlarges to hold the young animal in place. After several weeks, the joey becomes more active and gradually spends more and more time outside the pouch, which it leaves completely between 7 and 10 months of age.

(4) Kangaroos move by hopping on their powerful .... legs. They use their long, thick tail to balance the body while hopping. A kangaroo can hop at speeds of up to 60 kmh and can leap over .... up to 3 m high. Because of the unusual shape of its legs and its .... tail, a kangaroo cannot walk or move backwards very easily. Kangaroos are only found in Australia, Tasmania and New Guinea.

(5) As grazing animals, kangaroos eat grass, young shoots and leaves of plants and trees. Kangaroos need very little water to .... and are capable of going for months without drinking at all. The kangaroo usually rests in the shade during the day and comes out to eat in the late afternoon and night when it is much cooler.

(6) Kangaroos have good eyesight but only respond to moving objects. They have excellent hearing and can turn their large ears in all directions to pick up sounds. Kangaroos are social animals that live in groups or 'mobs' of up to 100 kangaroos.

4 Answer these questions about the different paragraphs from the text.

a Which paragraph tells you what food kangaroos eat?
b Which paragraph tells you what 'macropod' means?
c Which paragraph tells you about the kangaroo's sight and hearing?
d Which paragraph tells you how the kangaroo got its name?
e Which paragraph tells you where kangaroos live?
f Which paragraph tells you about young kangaroos?

5 Answer these questions.

   a Why was the kangaroo chosen as a symbol of Australia?
   b What are small species of kangaroo called?
   c What size is a kangaroo when it is born?
   d Where does a young kangaroo live during its first weeks?
   e How does a kangaroo keep its balance?
   f What do the unusually shaped legs and large tail of a kangaroo prevent it from doing?
   g What does a kangaroo usually do during the day?

Task 2

6 You are going to listen to a conservationist being interviewed about the world's smallest lizard, the Jaragua. Look at these questions and try to predict the answers before you listen to the interview.

   a What is special about the Jaragua lizard?
   b Where was the lizard discovered?
   c Why is finding this particular lizard so important?
   d Is it likely that a smaller lizard will be found in the near future?
   e What other small animals live in the Caribbean?
   f What problem faces the Caribbean's forest region?
   g What have local people done to secure the future of the Caribbean's environment?
   h What must the Jaragua lizard guard against?

7 Here are incomplete answers to the questions in Exercise 6. Match them correctly to the questions.

   a Because it's as …… as a land animal can be.
   b Birds, frogs and …… .
   c …… which may eat it.
   d It's the world's …… lizard.
   e …… .
   f Only …… remains and some species of animal may soon become …… .
   g The lizard was discovered in …… different …… .
   h They have formed …… organisations.

8 Listen to the text and complete the answers to the questions in Exercise 6.   Track 5

9 Write a short summary about the Jaragua lizard. Use the answers you wrote in Exercises 6 and 8.

Unit 14   63

Language focus

10 Complete the grid below with the words in the box taken from the interview you listened to. If you write the words in the correct space the shaded area will reveal a word which means 'our surroundings'.

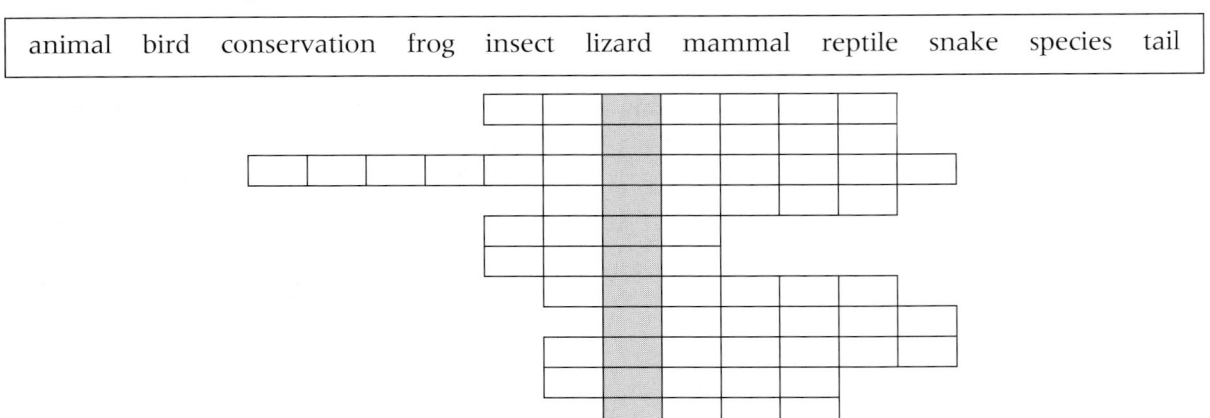

| animal   bird   conservation   frog   insect   lizard   mammal   reptile   snake   species   tail |

What is the word which means 'our surroundings'?

11 In unit 14 of the coursebook *should* and *would* are used like this:

…an appropriate memorial to her <u>should</u> be established. (used as an obligation)
If you <u>would</u> like to receive … (used as an offer)

They can also be used like this:

- *would* – to talk about past habits
- *should/would* – a mixed form which can be used for requests, offers and sentences with 'if'.

Identify the use of *should/would* in the following sentences.

  a 'Would you like a cup of tea?'
  b You *should* finish your homework now.
  c As a child he *would* walk to school.
  d If they read the newspapers they *would* understand more.

12 Write one sentence for each of the following:

  a *should* for obligation
  b *would* to talk about a past habit
  c a sentence where either *should* or *would* can be used equally
  d *would* with 'if'
  e *would* as an offer

13 Complete the following chart with words taken from the workbook texts.

	verb	past tense	past participle
a	discover		
b	find		
c	have		
d	know		
e	become		
f	say		
g	be		
h	cling		
i	compete		
j	take		
k	feed		

14 Write sentences using the verbs in any form from Exercise 13.

Example: **a**
Conservationists in the Caribbean <u>have discovered</u> the smallest lizard.

Vocabulary box

reptile

A 14th century word which originates from the Latin 'repere', which means 'to creep'.

Unit 15

In this unit you will have the opportunity to do some examination practice with exam practice questions. These will focus on the examination areas covered in the previous four coursebook units: exam exercises (reading & writing) 1, 2, 4, 5, 6 & 7 and listening.

Exam Exercise 1

Read the leaflet below (which is aimed mainly at western tourists) and then answer the questions which follow.

Weekend holiday breaks for all the family!

Middle East – Bahrain, Jordan, Kuwait, Lebanon, Oman, Qatar, Saudi Arabia, United Arab Emirates and Yemen

The mysteries of the east are waiting for you: from the ancient cities of Petra in Jordan to the oases in Saudi Arabia, there's always plenty to see and explore, and new experiences to be savoured.

For those seeking a holiday at any time of the year, the stunning beaches of Dubai in the United Arab Emirates are the place to be. Abu Dhabi is a modern city overflowing with wealth and vitality. Look for bargains in the gold market, and why not experience camel racing?

THINGS TO DO AND SEE
Jordan – Petra, spice route between Petra and Gaza
Oman – National Museum
Saudi Arabia – souks and markets
United Arab Emirates – gold market and souks, fine beaches, camel racing

Muscat is in the heart of Oman, a place to unwind and relax. Explore the fascinating castles, architectural sites, beaches, the old Muttrah souk, and discover more about Omani life in the city's National Museum.

HOTELS IN THE MIDDLE EAST

	Luxury*	Standard*
Jordan	$65	$37
Oman	$62	$38
Qatar	$75	$46
Saudi Arabia	$59	$42
UAE	$67	$47

*Prices are per person per night, based on two adults sharing a room, including breakfast. Single occupancy is charged at double the per person price.

Africa – Egypt, Eritrea, Gabon, Kenya, Morocco and Tunisia

The spice and variety of Africa is sure to appeal to everyone.

Egypt – visit the land of the ancient Pharoahs, follow the Nile from Cairo and be sure not to miss the Pyramids. Both the resorts of Sharm El Sheikh and Hurghada allow you to relax on the fine beaches. Try scuba diving and experience for yourself the beauty of the underwater world.

Morocco is full of eastern promise. Go to the markets and bargain for jewellery, carpets and rugs, and a whole selection of beautiful items. Casablanca is a modern city with a traditional Moorish heart where you won't want to miss the old palaces, peaceful gardens and enjoy the lively nightlife only Morocco can offer.

Kenya is for safaris. Look out for your favourite animals in their natural surroundings. Or shop for gifts in Nairobi.

Tunisia offers the chance for more sightseeing in the ancient walled town of Hammamet. Try the local cuisine or shop for a bargain.

Gabon offers plenty of local colour with beautiful beaches and its vast areas of rainforest full of wildlife. Nightlife is sophisticated with plenty to do, or visit the old quarter for a taste of local, traditional Africa.

HOTELS IN AFRICA

	Luxury*	Standard*
Egypt	$52	$25
Eritrea	$74	$41
Gabon	$60	$30
Kenya	$77	$48
Morocco	$72	$50

*Prices are per person per night, based on two adults sharing a room, including breakfast. Single occupancy is charged at double the per person price, except in Kenya where 50% is charged.

Call 00 800 22 333 444 and ask for 'Weekend Holiday Breaks' or visit our new website www.weekendholidays.com

a Give **two** examples of mysteries of the east.   [1]
b When is a good time to visit the beach in Dubai?   [1]
c How can you find out more about life in Oman?   [1]
d What is the cost of a standard room for one person in a Qatar hotel?   [1]
e In which country does the leaflet recommend trying scuba diving?   [1]
f In which **two** countries can you see animals?   [1]
g Where should you try local food?   [1]
h How can you get more information?   [1]

[Total: 8]

Exam Exercise 2

Read the article below and then answer the questions which follow.

Gardening in the palm of your hand

The palm tree symbolises everything about tropical climates. It adds beauty to landscapes, lines our roads and grows in our gardens. Many palms are now placed outside front doors, on balconies and inside the home to give an exotic feel to living space.

Palm trees in hot climates are easy to grow and cultivate. You will need a seed, the right soil mix, a fertiliser and plenty of irrigation. There are dozens of books to help you get started, but for those of us who choose not to go this far, there is help close at hand in the form of readymade palm trees to take home from your local garden centre.

The Green Desert garden centre spans more than 5,000 m² of land which contains an impressive collection of over 3,000 palm trees. The centre is owned and run by Ali Al Hamsa, who started the business nearly 20 years ago. He explained how to cultivate a palm tree from seed: 'You have to start before the spring. Place the palm seeds under three centimetres of special soil for them to germinate; in other words, so that they start to grow. This should be done early in the year, preferably in January or February, or early March, but it depends on the temperature. If you have enough water and good soil the palm will grow very quickly.'

Palm trees vary greatly in size. You can buy small ones for the house, or grow them larger for planting in the garden. Some will grow as high as 20 metres. There are more than 3,000 species of palm trees around the world, with more being discovered all the time. However, most garden centres will only stock a small number of different types, due to local climate conditions. The stock will also depend on local demand for different palms. The Green Desert offers three: a palm for the garden which produces dates; a second for the garden which does not have fruit; and the third is a smaller palm which is ideal for growing inside the home, or on a balcony.

Price varies enormously, and is based entirely on the height of the palm tree. Some palms at the garden centre are small, only 30–40 cm in height, but nothing under 1 metre is ever sold. This is because smaller palms are not yet established.

'Once a palm reaches about 100 cm, it will be well established and will be able to survive the move from the garden centre to someone's home or garden,' says Ali Al Hamsa. 'A tree which is not established may suffer during transportation from the garden centre environment, which it is used to, to its new home, whether indoors or in the garden. People who buy palm trees – in fact any plant from a garden centre – are often totally unaware of how a plant can suffer when it's moved. A common problem is that the plant is banged about in a car, causing the roots to loosen from the soil. This means that the plant can be starved of essential water. Another problem is that the leaves and branches may get knocked and broken, making the plant look damaged and ugly. Some plants may never recover from shocks like this!'

It is no surprise that palm trees have become increasingly popular in the home. Not only do they provide a tropical atmosphere, they have also proven to be tolerant of a wide range of interior conditions, from air-conditioning to central heating. They are practically maintenance free. Surprisingly, an established indoor palm needs only a little sunlight for its leaves to retain their colour; also, it needs only a little water once a week to survive. If the roots of a palm drink a lot of water, the plant will grow, but this is not ideal when the palm is grown indoors. Palm trees in a pot in the home are watered to keep them alive, not to make them grow bigger.

If you are wondering how a palm tree might improve the look of your garden, you should go to an expert for advice and instructions on what to buy and how to plant it. But remember that palm trees are able to grow to great heights in a comparatively small area of land. However, because they have only one branch, palm trees are very easy to control, and there are no leaves to clear up. Unlike the leaves on most other trees, palm leaves do not fall down, allowing us to enjoy the trees' subtle colours and textures whatever the season.

a Where do palm trees provide an exotic feel to living space? Give **three** examples. [1]
b What **three** items are required to grow a palm tree from seed? [1]
c In what **two** ways can you get help if you want to grow a palm tree? [1]
d What determines in which month a palm seed should be planted? [1]
e Why do garden centres only offer a small selection of different types of palm tree? [2]
f How is the price of a palm tree calculated? [1]
g Why are small palm trees not available to buy? [1]
h In what **two** ways can a plant suffer when it is damaged during transport? [2]
i Why are palm trees becoming increasingly popular in the home? Give **four** reasons. [2]
j What is the result of giving indoor palm trees too much water? [1]
k Give **two** advantages of growing palm trees in the garden. [1]

[Total: 14]

Exam Exercise 4

Read the article about Antarctica, and then complete the task below.

The ice land of Antarctica

The evolution of Antarctica can be traced back to as much as three billion years, an age which most of us find difficult to conceive. At that time, Antarctica did not exist as a separate continent, but was connected to the southern continents which we now recognise as South America and Australia. A mere 150 million years ago, the separation of the continents began, and only 70 million years ago, Antarctica became isolated. This was the time when land mammals began to populate all the continents of the world.

Today, Antarctica is covered by polar ice, but fossils show that the climate and geography once supported a far wider and more abundant plant and animal life than the few seedless plants and insects which remain. About two hundred million years ago, Antarctica was densely forested with trees and rainforest-type plants. During its next period of change, 80 to 100 million years ago, trees more suited to cooler temperatures began to flourish; as the continent continued its drift towards the South Pole, until about 4 million years ago, these trees slowly died out. Around one million years ago, Antarctica became glaciated, with the ice making the perfect environment for the fossilisation of reptiles, mammals and plants of all descriptions.

However, most of the continent's evolutionary record still lies buried deep beneath the ice, which makes up more than 95% of the surface area. Even experts have no idea what important treasures are concealed under the thick cover of ice, which in places is as much as two thousand metres. This, along with the difficult working conditions and the enormous expense of sending expeditions to the area, have for many years restricted geological knowledge of Antarctica. More recently, great advances have been made by geologists in mapping the continent, and it is now known that the continent's geology is far more complex than previously thought.

There have been no significant earthquakes in the Antarctic region, making it the 'quietest' continent in terms of earthquake movement. However, in 1977, an unusually large earth movement did take place, with a magnitude of 6.4. The centre of the tremor was in the Bellingshausen Sea, to the west of Antarctica. This led geologists to believe that the region may in fact be more susceptible to earthquakes than had previously been believed.

You are going to give a talk to your school/college friends about the evolution of Antarctica. You have decided to use some information from the article in your talk.

Make **two** short notes under each of these headings as a basis for your talk.

  a 3 billion years ago
  b Between 150 million and 70 million years ago
  c Between 5 and 1 million years ago
  d 1977 – today

[8]

Exam Exercise 5

Read the article about the game of chess. Write a summary explaining:

- the reasons why chess is not currently classified as a sport
- why people say that this situation should change.

Your summary should be about 100 words long, and you should use your own words as far as possible. [10]

The 'sport' of chess

After many years of failed attempts by the British Chess Federation (BCF) to have the game of chess classified as a sport, it seems that the situation is soon to change. Once a game has been officially recognised as a sport, its governing bodies are entitled to apply to the government for funds which can be used to promote the sport and provide support for the people who play it. Experts argue that because no public money is being invested in chess, there is a great deal of talent which is not being exploited.

Britain has always been one of the world's leading chess nations, but to continue to keep up with the best in the world, financial assistance is urgently needed. The equivalent of the BCF in Greece receives nearly half a million pounds from the Greek government each year.

The problem in classifying chess as a sport is that it does not meet all the necessary government criteria. Officially, chess is not 'physical' enough, but critics give the examples of snooker and motor racing, and point out that Formula One drivers even sit down to take part. The British government currently provides funds to a long list of sports, including arm wrestling, tug-of-war, skipping and sombo, a form of Russian wrestling; however, despite the fact that there are over three million players of chess in the UK, the government has never provided any financial aid.

As one of the most mentally challenging games in the world, leading professional chess players have to undergo months of physically demanding training before major competitions, which often include games of up to seven hours' duration. The International Olympic Committee is considering chess for inclusion in future Olympic competitions.

A fourteen-year-old girl from the UK, Jessie Gilbert, is a Chess Federation Master, having been the women's amateur chess champion at the age of eleven, two years after first learning to play the game. Jessie's parents estimate that it costs about £6,000 per year to keep her involved in chess: lessons, travel to competitions, computer databases for analysis of her rivals' tactics, books. Jessie says that because chess requires so much physical and mental effort, it is ridiculous that it is still not recognised as a sport.

Exam Exercise 6

Your English-speaking pen friend is going to visit your country for the first time. S/he will be coming to stay with you and your family.

Write her/him a letter in which you:

- describe your local area
- explain some interesting activities that you could do together
- suggest some places worth visiting

Begin your letter 'Dear ... '. (You do not need to write an address at the top.)

Your letter should be about 100–150 (core) / 150–200 (extended) words long.

Exam Exercise 7

You are the secretary of an environmental group at your school. Write an article for your monthly newsletter encouraging other students to join the group.

Your article should include the following areas:

- why you are worried about the environment
- the environmental problems in your area
- what students can do to improve the environment

Your letter should be about 100–150 (core) / 150–200 (extended) words long.

Listening exercise   Track 6

Listen to the talk about the future of DVDs, and then answer the questions below. You will hear the talk twice.

a	What does the writer say was the advantage of using records?	[1]
b	What have survived better than audio cassettes?	[1]
c	When did compact discs first become available?	[1]
d	Give **two** ways in which the storage capacity of a DVD can be increased.	[2]
e	What are the **two** disadvantages of using DVDs?	[2]

[Total: 7]

Unit 16

Task 1

You are going to read a newspaper article about Berlin, in Germany.

1 Before you read it, look at these notes about the city of Berlin. Write something similar about where you live. You can add other points if you wish.

Berlin	your home town
complex public transport system	
offers good night-time entertainment	
rich in history	
can eat out nearly any time of the day	
other points …	

2 Look at the words in the list. Put each one into the appropriate category. Give each category a title. Use your dictionary for help.

fare   Reichstag   clubs   cuisine   Palace of Princesses   trams   eaterie   U-Bahn
shopping   entertainment   S-Bahn   Olympic Stadium   tasty   restaurants

public transport	?	?	?
fare			

3 Find the words from Exercise 2 in the text below.

4 Read the text below and answer the questions.

Berlin: two in one

Berlin is one of the most interesting and exciting cities in the world. It is a true metropolis, with its own distinctive character and a vitality second to none. It has plenty to offer: culture, history, theatre and cinema, shopping, clubs, food, parks … the list is endless.

The public transport system in Berlin is exceptional, especially when you consider that two very different systems had to be combined after the Berlin Wall came down. The U-Bahn (underground train) has 9 lines, and the S-Bahn (suburban railway) serves all parts of the city. Street trams still run in the former east part of Berlin. The city is divided into three zones for the purpose of using the public transport system, and most destinations can be reached with a single fare ticket costing €2.10. Day tickets and 7-day tickets are also available.

Food in restaurants is generally available for up to 12 hours each day, starting from about midday. On every street corner you will find an eaterie of some description. German food is not well-known, but it is gaining in popularity. A very popular place with business people is the Berlin Restaurant, which offers international cuisine, as well as tasty local German dishes. The restaurant is beautifully decorated, and because of its high position the views over the city are wonderful.

Although there is plenty to do during the day, Berlin really comes alive at night. The free magazines *Flyer* and *030*, also available in bars and clubs all over Berlin, contain full details of everything that's happening. The busiest and most popular area of town is the Mitte, and Oranienburgerstrasse is the place to start your evening entertainment.

Berlin is synonymous with culture and history: the Berlin Wall, the Brandenburg Gate, Castle Bellevue, Checkpoint Charlie, to name but a few of the highlights. The Olympic Stadium was commissioned by Adolf Hitler for the Olympic Games which were held in Berlin in 1936; the Reichstag is once again the seat of the German government after years of exile in Bonn. The building is open to the public until midnight, although last entry is two hours earlier. Don't miss the Palace of Princesses, built in 1737 for the three daughters of Friedrich Wilhelm III, and the German Historical Museum, which dates back to 1695.

    a List the methods of public transport which are available in Berlin.
    b Apart from day tickets and 7-day tickets, which other type of public transport ticket can be used?
    c When does food generally stop being available in Berlin's restaurants?
    d Why was the Olympic Stadium originally built?
    e Where was the seat of German government before Berlin?
    f What is the latest time you can enter the Reichstag building?

Task 2

5 In Task 1 you read a passage about Berlin, which has changed considerably during the last 300 years. How do you think schools in your country will change over the next 50 years? Make notes on schools past, present and future.

	past	present	future
size of classrooms	very large – about 60 students	about 30 students	
location of schools			
facilities offered			
students' attitudes			
uniforms			
subjects taught			
teachers			

6 Look at the title of the text: *'Schools of the future' unveiled*

What does *unveiled* refer to here?

    – architectural plans have been uncovered
    – people have been told about secret future plans
    – students have given their ideas of how they want schools in the future

7 Match the words from the text in Column A to the correct meaning from the words/phrases in Column B. Use your dictionary for help.

A		B	
a	dome	i	built
b	variable	ii	different
c	piloted	iii	feelings
d	hexagonal	iv	changed
e	enhance	v	six-sided
f	morale	vi	hemisphere
g	impact	vii	out of the town centre
h	suburban	viii	effect
i	constructed	ix	tested
j	adjusted	x	strengthen

'Schools of the future' unveiled

The government has unveiled 11 designs for the 'schools of the future', with features including variable-sized classrooms and huge glass domes. The project, to be piloted in 14 areas, follows a competition in which 50 architects took part. The schools, expected to open from 2006, were designed to fit their settings – urban, rural or suburban.

An estimated 180 schools will be constructed as part of the Building Schools for the Future scheme, which will be extended nationwide. In inner-city areas, some schools will have streets running underneath them, in an effort to save space. Indoor courtyards will provide open spaces, while, for less built-up areas, architects have designed outdoor classrooms. These will link with sports areas.

One design for crowded urban areas – 'the honeycomb' – has hexagonal classrooms, which can be 'shaped like pieces of honeycomb, so they can interlock, wrap and enclose'.

The new schools are expected to have a working life of between 30 and 60 years. The size of the classrooms will be adjusted according to the number in the group being taught. Single-storey schools in countryside areas and multi-storey schools in towns will try to achieve the same light and airy effect, using materials which enhance sunlight. It is believed that this will improve morale amongst the students and so have a positive impact on educational standards. This is how the designs were chosen.

8 Answer the questions about the text using the given words.

    a What two examples of classroom design are given?
        The two examples …

    b How many schools are planned for the future?
        … are planned.

    c Why will some schools have streets underneath them?
        Schools …

    d What feature will schools in less built-up areas have?
        They will …

    e What is special about the size of the classrooms?
        That …

    f What is believed will help the students' morale?
        A …

    g How is it thought the buildings will affect standards of education?
        It is …

    h How long are the schools expected to be used for?
        They …

Language focus

9 In the text about Berlin we see:

    …destinations <u>can</u> be reached … (paragraph 2)
    …you <u>will</u> find an eaterie … (3)

The underlined words are both examples of modal auxiliary verbs, which are used before the verb in the infinitive and without 'to'. Other examples are *could, may, might, would, should* and *must*. As with all auxiliary verbs, modals in some way affect the meaning of the main verb.

Complete the sentences below using an appropriate modal. Some modals will need to be negative. Is there a choice of negative in any of the sentences?

    a He's just been ill with a bad cold so he … be swimming today.
    b You … invite them, but don't you think it will be too many people?
    c You really … get those presents sorted; it's nearly her birthday.
    d He … fail this exam; otherwise he won't get his promotion.
    e You … have got here on time if you had got the earlier bus.
    f It … be worth checking how much bread we've got, in case we run out later.
    g Do you think it's going to rain? … we take an umbrella?
    h She … be at work now because she always goes early on a Tuesday.

10 Make sentences of your own using these modal verbs.

    a could
    b might
    c shouldn't
    d mustn't
    e may
    f can't
    g won't
    h couldn't

11 In the texts in unit 16 of the coursebook the verbs *said, added* and *says* are used. Here are some other verbs you might see instead of *said*.

advised   moaned   shouted   suggested   joked   asked   answered   ordered   demanded

Make sentences of your own using these nine verbs. Use your dictionary for help.

12 In Column A are words which are opposite in meaning to words in the text *Get the msg?* in unit 16 of the coursebook. Write the words in Column B.

A	B
last	first
receiving	
emptied	
retreat	
tiny	
coming in	
informal	
same	
shrinking	
exactly	

13 Use the words from Exercise 12 to write meaningful sentences.

Vocabulary box

computer

Amazingly, this word comes from the Latin 'computare'. 'Com'= with/together and 'putare' = to consider/think.

Unit 17

Task 1

1 How healthily do you eat? Write down everything that you ate yesterday.

> **Yesterday I ate ...**
>
> *a cheese sandwich ...*

2 Do this quiz to find out if you do eat healthily or not. Use the list of things you ate yesterday to help.

a How many portions of fruit did you eat yesterday?	b How many portions of bread, other cereals and potatoes did you eat yesterday?	c How many portions of crisps, cakes or chocolate did you eat yesterday?
d How many portions of meat, fish and pulses did you eat yesterday?	e How much water did you drink yesterday?	f How many portions of milk or dairy products did you eat yesterday?

3 Use the following information to check how healthily you eat. The letters **a**, **b**, **c** etc. match the categories **a**, **b**, **c** etc. in Exercise 2.

  a You should eat at least 5 portions of fruit and vegetables every day. They contain vitamins and minerals that can help reduce the risk of heart disease and certain cancers.
  b Anything from 5 to 11 portions in this category is fine. Increasing your consumption of these starchy foods will help to reduce the amount of fat and increase the amount of fibre in your diet.
  c Try to limit yourself to 2 portions a day. It's important to enjoy you food and these are special treats, so you shouldn't worry about eating them if you have a balanced diet.
  d 2 to 3 portions a day makes a balanced diet. These foods are excellent sources of protein, which is needed for growth and repair.
  e You should drink about 2 litres of water every day. The human body is mostly water, so drinks are very important to keep our fluid intake correct.
  f You should aim for 2 to 3 portions of dairy products a day. They are essential for the development of bones and teeth.

4 Summarise the points above.

  Example:
  a *Fruit can reduce the risk of certain illnesses.*

Task 2

5 Look at these facts and figures:

60% of all 14–15 year old girls say they want to lose weight.
25% of 14–15 year old boys say they want to lose weight.

Answer these questions:

– Why do young people want to lose weight?
– What influences would make a young person unhappy with their body?
– What would you do if you thought your friend had eating problems?

6 Scan the text below and find the words required.

Example:
Find a word in paragraph 1 that means 'illnesses'.   *disorders*

a Find a word in paragraph 1 that means 'important'.
b Find a phrase in paragraph 2 that means 'poor image of self'.
c Find a phrase in paragraph 2 that means 'demands from own age group'.
d Find a word in paragraph 2 that means 'reasons'.
e Find a word in paragraph 3 that means 'unwilling'.
f Find a word in paragraph 3 that means 'finding out what is wrong'.
g Find a phrase in paragraph 4 that means 'picture of oneself'.
h Find a word in paragraph 5 that means 'aware'.
i Find a word in paragraph 6 that means 'accept'.
j Find a word in paragraph 6 that means 'real'.

Eating disorders

(1) It is very hard to tell the exact figures because no government health department or agency has collected any statistics on eating disorders for either young males or young females. It has been shown that males are open to the same disease causes as young females and that more males are suffering than ever before. It is being noted that there are small but significant increases.

(2) The main cause of these diseases is low self-esteem. Males face similar peer pressure with regard to body image and looks that young women do. They are also teased and bullied for being overweight and have problems with girlfriends/boyfriends and have schoolwork stresses. These are all important factors.

(3) Young males have traditionally been shy of talking about their problems. They are more reluctant to seek treatment and explain their feelings to parents and friends. Doctors have also had problems diagnosing the diseases in males. If a male has a well-muscled body and does a lot of exercise, then it is hard for a doctor to diagnose an eating disorder.

(4) But thanks to increased public information and awareness, boys are realising that they can finally talk about this issue. There has also been an increase in doctors' diagnoses. They are becoming much more aware of the warning signs. Another factor is the increase in the importance to young males of one of the disease causes – body image.

(5) Males are increasingly becoming self-conscious about their looks. This cause of the disease in males is much more obvious than ever before. The number of gyms trying to attract young males through their doors has vastly increased in numbers. Body-building has been proven as a cause of eating disorders.

(6) It is important for sufferers to acknowledge and recognise that they have a problem. They also have to have a genuine desire to get better as any treatment will require hard work and will be a lengthy process.

7 Look at the text and find evidence for the following statements.

Example:
Boys don't like to talk about themselves.
Young males have traditionally been shy … (paragraph 3)

    a Doctors are learning to see when the problem is getting dangerous.
    b They need to really want to improve.
    c There is no real evidence of dieting illnesses.
    d Boys are influenced by their friends.
    e A boy's strong-looking body makes it difficult to see there is a problem.
    f Numbers are going up.

8 Answer these questions based on the text.

    a Why is it difficult to give exact figures for eating disorders amongst teenagers?
    b What reason is given for why boys have eating disorders?
    c What don't boys like to talk about?
    d What haven't doctors been able to do up till now?
    e Why do boys now realise they can talk about their problem?
    f In what ways are gyms a problem?
    g What ways are suggested for dealing with the problem?

Language focus

9 Look at how the word *however* is used in the passage *The North Pole* in unit 17 of your coursebook:

This year, however, he was able to take … (paragraph 2)
However, it is true … (paragraph 10)

Both examples show how one idea contrasts with another. Other ways of expressing contrast are: *nevertheless, in spite of, on the other hand*.

Examples:
The company increased its profits this year. Nevertheless, salaries were not increased.
In spite of the cold, they decided to go for a walk.

Complete these sentences with a suitable 'contrast' form.

a Temperatures are higher this year …
b He studied very hard …
c She worked very hard until late last night …
d … they ran out of petrol.
e People on the island are extremely friendly …
f She speaks at least four languages …
g His doctor told him to go on a strict diet …
h The team played very well all year …

10 Complete the categories. Give yourself one minute to find as many words as you know.

fruit	dairy products	liquids	meat/fish	cereals
bananas	cheese	cola		

11 Based on the information in this unit, write **six** pieces of advice to someone who wants to improve their diet. Use *should* in each of the sentences.

Example:
You <u>should</u> eat at least five pieces of fruit or vegetables every day.

12 Look at the lists of words. Decide which word in each group does not belong and state why.

Example:
butter milk <u>eggs</u> cheese. Eggs are not a product made from milk.

a banana cherry melon apple
b beef veal chicken mutton
c polar bear penguin snow tiger elephant
d cow buffalo donkey cat
e India Pakistan Bangladesh China
f monsoon floods drought rain

13 Look at the words in Exercise 12.

a Which word also means 'hen'?
b Which is a domestic animal?
c What do cows give us?
d Which country's capital city is Delhi?
e What can be eaten green and are known as plantains?
f What is similar to a horse?
g Deserts always have these.
h Which bird cannot fly?

Vocabulary box

desert

This is a 12th century word originally from the Latin 'desertum', which means 'abandoned place'. Sahara, as in the Sahara desert, comes from the Arabic 'sahra' and simply means 'desert'.

Unit 18

Task 1

1 Are there any single-sex schools (schools where there are either *only* boys or *only* girls at the school – not mixed) where you live? Give reasons why you would or would not like to go to a single-sex school.

would like	would not like

2 What do you think are the advantages and disadvantages of single-sex schools?

advantages	disadvantages

3 Look at this statement taken from the text you are going to read. What do you think it means?

When girls go to a single-sex school, they stop being the audience and become the players.

4 You are now going to read the text *Why a girls' school?* What information do you think the text will contain?

Write **three** ideas.

Example:
Teachers may expect more from girls.

5 Skim the text and tick off any of your ideas from Exercise 4 that you find.

82   Unit 18

Why a girls' school?

The school is the first all-girls school in this area. The founding of the school was based on current research, which demonstrates that many girls attending co-educational (i.e. girls and boys together) schools do not receive equal opportunities to excel academically and socially. Girls' self-esteem and confidence in their abilities, particularly with regard to maths and science, fall during the middle school years, narrowing their later choices of college work and career paths.

It has been shown that girls in co-educational classrooms often have to battle against:

– fewer opportunities to participate
– lowered teacher expectations
– limited encouragement in maths and science
– unequal sports opportunities
– insufficient female role models
– pressure to conform to stereotypes

In contrast, at a girls' school, girls find out not about equal opportunities, but about every opportunity. Girls experience the freedom to speak out, ask questions, debate issues, and defend points of view. Girls fill every role at an all-girls school: they are the speakers, thinkers, writers, singers, artists, scientists, athletes, actors and leaders. When girls go to a single-sex school, they stop being the audience and become the players.

We know that girls at single-sex schools do well academically. In general, graduates of girls' schools are more motivated, more accomplished and have higher ambitions than their peers at co-educational schools. They plan careers in maths, science and technology four times more often than their peers from other schools. They score 30% higher in tests than the girls' national average. In addition, almost 100% of girls' schools graduates go on to college and are twice as likely to earn doctorates.

6 Find where in the text these ideas are. State on which line each one can be found.

Example:
Girls tend to go on to higher education.   line 22

a Girls are more likely to apply for subjects that they would not traditionally choose.
b They perform better in examinations.
c As girls become older they are less sure of their abilities.
d Teachers don't expect them to do as well.
e Girls have more chance to express themselves.
f Girls are more ambitious when they finish school.
g They don't have the same chances in mixed schools.
h There are fewer chances for them to get involved when it is a co-educational school.

Task 2

7 Look at this exam practice question:

> Some people say that educating boys and girls separately produces much better results.
>
> Write an article for your school or college magazine in which you give your opinion about this.
>
> The comments below may give you some ideas but you are free to use ideas of your own.
>
> > 'Without boys and girls together, how can we discuss real issues?'
> >
> > 'I find that boys can be very disruptive in class, so I prefer not having them around.'
> >
> > 'It's not natural to be separated in this way.'
> >
> > 'Having girls in the classroom with boys calms us down and makes us study harder.'
>
> **Your article should be about 150–200 words long.**

Think back to the previous units which focused on writing. How will you approach this question? What stages do you need to go through? Discuss with your partner and make a list.

8 Look at these two sample introductory paragraphs to the question above. Which do you think is the better introduction? Why?

Student A

I don't think that separating boys and girls at school is a good idea because we can both learn a lot from each other. Girls sometimes have a much better idea about things than we do and so if they are together with us in the classroom we can learn a lot of things from them.

Student B

The topic of whether to educate girls and boys together is a complex one, and I believe that there are many things to be considered. Personally, I am in favour of co-education, but I can understand the views of those who support single-sex education.

9 Write your own introductory paragraph to the question. Before you start, think carefully about what information should go into the introduction.

10 Look at these two sample concluding paragraphs to the question above. Which do you think is the better conclusion? Why?

Student C

On balance, I think we need to continue to educate boys and girls separately. Despite the reservations outlined above, I believe that until we can guarantee the same or better results with boys and girls being educated together, we should not change the current situation.

Student D

It is my opinion that we should be in class together because we can learn from each other, we can have more fun, we can help each other, and so on.

11 Write your own concluding paragraph to the question. Before you start, think carefully about what information should go into the conclusion.

12 Answer this exam practice question:

> Your headteacher has decided that all students in your school must take part in competitive team sports.
>
> Write an essay in which you give your opinion about compulsory competitive team sports in your school.
>
> The comments below may give you some ideas but you are free to use ideas of your own.
>
> > *'Playing with your friends and against your friends can be confusing.'*
> > *'I like the chance to play together – we never do it otherwise.'*
> > *'This focus on competition and always having a winner is not healthy.'*
> > *'Who cares about winning and losing? Why can't we just have some fun?'*
>
> **Your essay should be about 150–200 words long.**

Language focus

13 Look at these sentences from the text *Gum disease* in unit 18 of the coursebook:

And anti-smoking groups would rather see people chewing than smoking.

Would rather means 'would prefer to' and is followed by the verb in the infinitive without 'to'.

We often use the contracted form *'d rather*.

Example:
I'd rather stay if you don't mind

We can also use *would rather* + subject + past tense.

Example:
I'd rather you visited her later.

This is used to show preference in an action.

Write sentences using the forms above for the following situations:

Example:
You don't want to stay late at a party.
I'd rather we came home earlier.

a A friend wants you to lend him some money but you don't want to.
   b You don't want to go for a walk as you want to watch TV.
   c You don't want to eat the food that has been cooked for you.
   d You want to go to the cinema and not to the theatre.
   e You have to choose a day to visit a friend.
   f You've been told to make a speech but you don't want to.

14 Look at the text on page 137 of your coursebook *A little pick-me-up...* and find words which have the same meaning as those in Column A. Write the equivalent word in Column B. Do not worry about the other columns yet.

A	B	C	D
huge shop	hypermarket		
come out			
unusual			
doctor			
lucky			
the jobless			
apartments			
cellar			
rules			
piled			
broken			
impossible			

15 Write the words you have in Column B in the correct alphabetical order in Column C.

16 Cover up Columns A, B and C. How many of the words can you remember? Write them with the correct spelling in alphabetical order in Column D. When you have finished, check to see if all the words are correctly written.

Vocabulary box

pavement

This is a 13th century word which is originally from the Latin word 'pavimentum', meaning 'a beaten floor'. This comes from 'pavire', which means 'to beat' or 'to tread down'. US English uses the word 'sidewalk', which has a more literal meaning.

Unit 19

Task 1

1. Imagine you wish to work in the world of fashion. What different jobs do you think would be available in this area of work? List them in the first column. Do not worry about the second column yet.

Example: *fashion buyer*	
a	
b	
c	
d	
e	

2. How does your list match with the one below? In the second column, tick off those which you have listed – did you find any different ones?

   a fashion buyer
   b store manager
   c fashion photographer
   d costume designer
   e fashion designer
   f graphic designer
   g fashion journalist
   h public relations

3. Match the jobs in Exercise 2 with a description below.

Whether in a studio or on location, you could be the person who takes the pictures.	c
You go to the show, chat with the designers, then write about it all for the magazines.	
If you think you can manage all the publicity and photo-calls of top models and designers then this could be the job for you.	
Put your imagination and artistic talent to good use and you could be the person behind the look of magazines.	
Want to take control of which clothes appear on the shelves of your favourite store? Going to the top fashion houses to buy the latest fashion could be the job for you.	
Want to style the stars? Think you can make your friends dress to impress?	
If you would love to manage a team and have an interest in and love of fashion – this could be perfect for you.	
Do you love theatre and musicals and think you would enjoy researching, designing and making costumes for shows?	

4. Which job appeals to you most? Give **four** reasons why you would like to do it.

5. Which job appeals to you least? Give **four** reasons why you wouldn't like to do it.

Task 2

You are going to listen to an interview with someone who is a marketing assistant in the fashion world.

6 Before you listen, decide if you think these statements are true (T) or false (F).

- A lot of work experience will help you get a job.
- Making contacts is very important in the fashion industry.
- Having a university degree is not important.
- It's important to meet deadlines.
- People remember other people who are confident.
- You should try to focus on one particular area of the fashion business.

7 You will hear these words/phrases in the interview. What do they mean? Match them to the definitions opposite. Use your dictionary for help.

8 Look at these questions. Before you listen to the interview, identify the key words in each question.

A	B	
a PA	**i**	choices
b relevant	**ii**	connected
c retail	**iii**	personal assistant
d vital	**iv**	changeable
e deadline	**v**	very important
f invaluable	**vi**	time something must be completed by
g fickle	**vii**	sale of goods
h options	**viii**	up to date
i on the pulse	**ix**	necessary

  a Where did the person being interviewed see the advert for the first job?
  b What was the second job she applied for?
  c What **two** things helped her get the second job?
  d What **three** examples does she give of how going to university helped her?
  e Why does she say work experience is important?
  f What does she say you should always be on the look out for?
  g What shouldn't you do when you begin a job?
  h Why does she say reading magazines will help in your job?

9 Listen and answer the questions in Exercise 8.   Track 7

10 How many of the statements from Exercise 6 did you guess correctly?

Language focus

11 Look at how *whether ... or* is used in this sentence from the unit:

<u>Whether</u> in a studio <u>or</u> on location, you could be the person who takes the pictures.

Here is another example:

<u>Whether</u> you go in my car <u>or</u> in hers, you are going to be late.

Write **five** sentences using *whether ... or*.

12 What is the difference in meaning between the pairs of words below? Use your dictionary for help.

Example:
<u>newspaper / magazine</u>
A newspaper usually comes out every day and normally covers all types of news.
A magazine deals with specific areas and is normally weekly or monthly.

- **a** retailing / buying
- **b** marketing / selling
- **c** styling / designing
- **d** career / job
- **e** picture / photograph
- **f** industry / factory
- **g** shy / nervous
- **h** confident / brave

13 Complete the grid below, selecting words from Exercise 12. You will find a word connected to this unit.

- **a** opposite in meaning to 'g'
- **b** a job for a lifetime
- **c** could mean 'embarrassed'
- **d** picture taken with a camera
- **e** opposite of selling
- **f** place where things are produced
- **g** you might feel like this before an exam or job interview

a												
b												
c												
d												
e												
f												
g												

14 These words are related to the fashion industry. Use your dictionary to find out what they mean.

    a cat-walk
    b chic
    c accessories
    d haute couture
    e designer wear
    f look
    g fashionistas

Vocabulary box

fashion

This is a 14th century word which comes indirectly from the French 'façon', which means 'shape'. Its root is the Latin 'facere', which means 'to make'.

Unit 20

This is a complete sample examination for you to practise your technique. Your teacher will tell you exactly what to do.

Exam Exercise 1

Read the advertisement below about 'Ecoworld', and then answer the questions which follow.

Ecoworld Discovery Centre

The future is here at Ecoworld Discovery Centre!

+ Eco class for children!
Hands-on interactive games, challenging and fun! Discover the environmental world in an exciting and educational way. Special activities for different ages.

+ Eco organic gardens!
Find out how to protect the environment in your own back garden! Learn practical and exciting tips to follow at home. Find out what lives under the grass and in the trees! Children under 8 supervised by special helpers.

+ Eco wind turbine!
Climb the 500 steps to the top of the 85 metre wind turbine tower and see the amazing view of Carlstown and the river beyond. For a small extra charge, go on a special tour of the machine room (children under 12 not allowed without an adult).

+ Eco gift shop and Eco restaurant!
Amazing gifts for all the family, each one specially chosen by our team of eco experts! The Eco restaurant has a great choice of snacks and drinks, with a wide range of vegetarian dishes available. There is access for wheelchair users to both the gift shop and the restaurant, and large print food menus for sight-impaired visitors. Picnic area and free parking every day.

KIDS – Special meals at reduced prices!

Opening times:
April 1st – September 30th : Monday – Friday 10am – 6pm, Weekends closes one hour later
October 1st – March 31st : Monday – Friday closed, Weekends 10am – 4pm
Public holidays – closed
School groups:
Weekdays October 1st – March 31st : 10am – 2pm. Booking essential.

Tel: 01882 – 733092, Fax: 01882 – 733093

a Where in the Ecoworld Discovery Centre can children of different ages do different activities? [1]
b Where can you learn about things which live and grow outdoors? [1]
c What can you see from the top of the tower? Give **two** things. [1]
d What do you have to do if you want to visit the machine room? [1]
e Give **three** ways in which Ecoworld hopes to encourage parents to bring their young children. [2]
f Give **three** pieces of information about the restaurant. [1]
g At what time does the centre close on a Sunday in July? [1]

[Total: 8]

Exam Exercise 2

Read the following article, and then answer the questions below.

A day in the mountains

The Troodos area of Cyprus is only an hour's drive from the coast, so why not consider a day trip up into the mountains as a refreshing change from the beach? It will also be a wonderful opportunity to get away from the traffic and noise of the city and to breathe in some clean, pine-scented air while enjoying stunning views.

The Troodos mountains are the ideal location for hikers, bikers, nature lovers and skiers, as well as for those who simply want to picnic. If you want to ski, remember that the runs are not very long; however, the skiing facilities are excellent. Troodos is often said to be a good place to learn to ski because the slopes are not too demanding.

The impressive Troodos range of mountains with its rugged scenery and vast pine and cedar forests stretches across most of the western side of Cyprus. The summit of Mount Olympus stands at 1,950 m and offers panoramic views. Keen walkers and hikers will enjoy the nature trails laid out, which include carefully signposted information on the trees, flowers and shrubs encountered on the trail. The longest of these trails is the circular 12 km Atlantic Trail, which goes around Olympus at an altitude of about 1,700 to 1,750 m, with outstanding views of the whole island. There are over 120 endemic plants and flowers in the Troodos mountain range, including peonies, rockroses and orchids.

There are many important churches and monasteries in the mountains, including nine Byzantine painted churches, which are UNESCO World Heritage listed sites. The best-known monastery is the Monastery of Kykko, home to a very important icon, reputedly painted by Saint Luke. The tomb of Archbishop Makarios III, the first president of Cyprus, is nearby, looking towards the village of Panayia, where he was born.

The rustic charm of the mountain villages must be experienced and, if you go at the right time of the year, you will be able to buy cherries, plums, apples, grapes and pears, which are all at their freshest and best in the mountains. Each mountain village has its own special charm; perhaps you will try to fit in a number of these, and save others for your next visit. The village of Agros is famous for its aromatic rosewater, an important ingredient in the mouth-watering local cuisine. Kakopetria, at the head of the Solea valley, is well known for its excellent restaurants and beautifully renovated village houses. Lania is known as the village of the artists, while Platres is a hillside resort with a friendly atmosphere, and numerous hotels and shops. Nearby are the perennial Caledonian Falls. Phoini, a village 4 km west of Platres, is famous for its pottery and trout farm.

If you are near the magnificent Cedar valley, you might also catch a glimpse of the Cyprus moufflon, the wild sheep which is endemic to Cyprus and whose male is characterised by large, sickle-shaped horns. The moufflon is an inhabitant of the mountainous Paphos Forest, which covers 60,000 hectares in the west of the island. It is a protected species and due to its tragic past, when it was hunted almost to extinction, some moufflon now live in protected enclosures. Here they can be admired without disturbing their peace.

a   Why is it worth thinking about a day trip to the mountains? [1]
b   Other than getting away from the noise and traffic in the town, what **two** other benefits of the mountains are mentioned? [2]
c   Who are the Troodos mountains ideal for? Give **four** examples. [1]
d   Give **two** reasons why Troodos is a good place for beginners to ski. [2]
e   Where in Cyprus are the mountains? [1]
f   What information can mountain walkers find? [1]
g   How high is the longest mountain trail? [1]
h   What can be found in the mountains, other than plants and animals? [1]
i   Why is the village of Panayia important? [1]
j   What is sold in the mountain villages at certain times of the year? [1]
k   In which **two** villages is good food guaranteed? [1]
l   Why is the moufflon a protected species? [1]

[Total: 14]

Exam Exercise 3

Read the following passage about Kadil Adallan and then complete the tasks which follow.

Kadil Adallan is 16 years old and is currently attending the Capital School. The school's contact details are as follows: telephone and fax 246815, email capitalschool@arabianet.net, website www.capitalschool.ac.om. Kadil lives at 46 Ruwi Street, Muscat, Oman. He does not have a telephone at home, but his mother's work telephone is 246993. Kadil checks his emails on a computer at school, and his email address is kadilrunner@hotmail.com.

Kadil is a very keen sprint athlete who has already represented his school in a number of events, including the 100 and 200 metre races. Two years ago he won the Oman under-15 200 metre race. He has also recently won an inter-school 100 metre race for students.

The municipality of Salalah (in the south of Oman, about 1,000 km from the capital, Muscat) is organising a sports day for students, and Kadil has decided to enter. The event takes place on 27 June. There is an entry fee of $28 for under-16s, and $45 for 16 and over, which must be sent with the application form. Kadil thinks this is too expensive and he is hoping to find someone who will sponsor him. The organisers of the sports day want to attract as many sponsors as possible in order to raise money for children with special educational needs.

The closing date for applications is only three days away. Kadil has decided to ask his local sports club if they will pay his entry fee. His trainer at the club is Mrs Fatima Indiri, her address is 719 Salalah Road, Muscat, and her telephone number is 246114.

As Kadil does not live in Salalah, he will need transport to the sports day, and accommodation. There is a regular bus service between Muscat and Salalah which costs $20 for a single ticket and $30 for a return. Students pay half price. The overnight journey takes 12 hours, departing from Muscat at six o'clock in the evening. The return bus from Salalah leaves at seven o'clock in the morning. Gulf Air operates flights between Muscat and Salalah, and further information about times and prices is available from the event organisers. Kadil will get the bus on 25 June and return to Muscat on 28 June. The ticket money must be included with the application form.

Accommodation is available in the Salalah Hotel. A single room costs $75 per night, including breakfast. Kadil will need to pay for the hotel when he checks in. Lunch and dinner are provided by the organisers, and they have to be notified of any special dietary requirements. Kadil will need a room at the hotel for 2 nights, and he does not have any particular food requirements. Salalah municipality is offering a choice of entertainment on 27 and 28 June. Kadil would like to watch a film about famous athletes, or attend an exhibition about Omani culture.

Salalah sports day

Application Form

SECTION A – please complete in block capitals
Surname: Initial: Age:
Male/Female (please delete as appropriate)
Home address:
Telephone: Email:

SECTION B
Running experience & competitions entered:
Name & address of proposed sponsor:
Telephone: Email:

SECTION C
Arrival date and time: …   …
Departure date and time: …   …
Do you require transport?   YES   NO
Type of transport: bus   plane
Type of ticket (return / single):   …
Ticket price enclosed: $ …
Entry fee enclosed: $28 $45
Do you require accommodation?   YES   NO
Number of nights: …
Special food requirements (please list):   …
Entertainment (please tick first and second choices):
27 June   ☐ basketball   ☐ film night   ☐ beach walk   ☐ exhibition
28 June   ☐ volleyball   ☐ exhibition   ☐ shopping   ☐ film night

SECTION D
Write **one** sentence of 12–20 words telling us why you think your application to join our sports day should be accepted.

Exam Exercise 4

Read the following article about whaling, and then answer the task which follows.

The history of whaling

Whales have been hunted for nearly two thousand years, mainly for food but also as a source of fuel and material for making tools and weapons. The first whale hunters were Eskimos and American Indians, but in the 15th century whales were also hunted in the seas off western Europe. Whalers from France and Spain ventured far from home in their pursuit of whales, some travelling as far as Iceland.

Later on in the 17th century, Dutch and English fishermen built large fleets of whaling ships, having realised the enormous value of whale products. It is estimated that at times the Dutch had 300 ships at sea with more than 18,000 sailors on board. In the early 18th century, these fleets of ships were forced to hunt as far away as Greenland, as the number of whales closer to home decreased rapidly due to over-whaling. Towards the end of the 18th century, brick ovens were installed on whaling ships. These ovens allowed whalers to boil and process the precious whale blubber or fat at sea and store it in barrels, rather than stopping frequently at ports in order to offload supplies. This meant that whaling ships commonly stayed at sea for up to four years before returning home with their cargo.

During the 19th century, the Pacific and Arctic Oceans became the new hunting grounds. A fleet of more than 700 whaling ships from the USA dominated the world industry, which demanded more and more whale products up until the end of the century. With the rise of the petroleum industry, the need for whale blubber decreased rapidly, but the 20th century saw a dramatic rise in new uses for whale products.

The original Eskimo whalers sailed in skin boats and used harpoons to kill whales, which were attached to long ropes also made of skin. European and North American whalers used similar methods. Usually six men in a boat about 9 m long would go after a whale. The boat was equipped with harpoons and long ropes. A whaler would throw the harpoon and, once hit, the whale would swim away underwater, then resurface as it became exhausted, when it would be harpooned again. The whale was then strapped to the side of the boat, its fat would be removed, and the rest of the body would be thrown away.

In the mid 19th century, a gun was developed that fired harpoons which contained a small explosive charge. The gun could throw the harpoon much greater distances than a man, and this meant that faster-swimming whales could now be hunted.

Nowadays, helicopters, sonar and high-powered harpoon guns, as well as other technology, have made the whaling industry able to catch enormous quantities of whales. Whaling ships now have on-board equipment and laboratories for processing whales, which means that a whale as big as a prehistoric dinosaur can be completely processed in less than an hour.

You are going to give a talk to your school/college about the history of whaling.

You have decided to use some information from the article in your talk.

Make **two** short notes under each of these headings as a basis for your talk.

- a 15th – 17th centuries
- b 18th century
- c 19th century
- d present day   [8]

Exam Exercise 5

Read the following article about cyclones. Write a summary in which you include:

- information about the wind speed of cyclones
- the location of cyclones.

Your summary should be about 100 words long, and you should use your own words as far as possible.

Extreme weather – the cyclone

Cyclones form as tropical depressions above warm sea water, and usually cover a huge area, often between 200 and 400 kilometres across. The majority of tropical depressions never actually reach the stage of becoming a cyclone, and simply lose their strength over a period of some days. Those that do become tropical cyclones may live for between a few hours and several weeks, but most last from five to ten days.

Wind speed

In the early stages of a tropical storm the wind increases in strength from 'weak storm' status (65–87 kph) to gale-force status (up to 118 kph), which is typical of the speed of a tropical cyclone. The wind spirals towards a distinct centre, called the 'eye', which can be anything from five to fifteen kilometres in diameter. As the wind speed of the spiral increases, atmospheric pressure drops rapidly, and the diameter of the eye may increase to as much as 200 kilometres. Many tropical storms will not actually develop any further than this, and while there may be occasional wind speeds in excess of 120 kph, the storms never actually become tropical cyclones.

Travel over land

Cyclones which travel over a land surface lose a considerable amount of their energy and wind speed due to the friction created with the land contours. In mountainous areas of Vietnam, most cyclones die out very quickly; however, in the flat plateau areas of Western Australia, there is little in the natural geography to create the friction necessary to reduce the strength of a cyclone. Cyclones in this area commonly travel more than 1,500 kilometres. In 1969 in the United States, hurricane 'Camille' travelled 1,800 kilometres, and while it lost much of its strength, it kept its structure.

Location

Nowadays, every cyclonic disturbance is detected by satellite. The major areas in the North Atlantic are: south of the Cape Verde Islands, east of the Lesser Antilles, the western Caribbean Sea and the Gulf of Mexico. Water temperatures in the latter two areas rise quickly in the early summer months, causing cyclones to evolve before other areas. As water temperatures rise to 28°C and more in late July and August, the number of cyclones across the Atlantic area increases. The storms travel west, gathering strength, and then curve back. By mid- to late-September, as water temperatures begin to cool, the area of cyclone origin returns to the Caribbean and the Gulf of Mexico.

[10]

Exam Exercise 6

COMPETITION

YOUNG SPORTS WRITER

We would like you to tell us about a sports event you have recently attended.
What was the sport? Where did it take place?
Why did you go? Why was it memorable?
Write us a short article.
Fantastic prizes to be won!
Best entries will be printed in the newspaper!

You have just read this announcement in a newspaper and have decided to enter the competition.

Write your entry.

Your article should be about 100–150 (core) / 150–200 (extended) words long.

Don't forget to include:

- where you went and what the sports event was
- why you went
- why you have chosen to write about it.

You will receive up to 9 marks for the content of your article and up to 9 marks for the style and accuracy of your language.

Exam Exercise 7

Here are some different views on using animals for medical research:

> It is wrong to harm or kill animals just to help people – animals have feelings too!
>
> *It is essential that we test new medicines on animals before using them on people. What else can we do?*
>
> I think we should only use animals for things which will not harm them, such as beauty products.
>
> There is no excuse for testing lipstick and other makeup on animals. People do not need makeup! If we need to test new products, we should test them on ourselves.

Write an article for your school magazine explaining what you think about using animals for medical research.

The comments above may give you some ideas but you are free to use any ideas of your own.

Your article should be about 100–150 (core) / 150–200 (extended) words long.

You will receive up to 9 marks for the content of your article and up to 9 marks for the style and accuracy of your language.

Tapescript

Unit 4 (Track 1)

Listen to this interview with a spokesperson from the Food Advertising Unit and complete the notes in your workbook. You will hear the interview twice.

M1 Hello, and welcome to our weekly radio programme on advertising. Today we have here in the studio Margarita Assudo, spokesperson for the Food Advertising Unit.

F1 Hello.

M1 Margarita, what do parents and adults think about advertising to children?

F1 Advertising to kids, and particularly food advertising to kids, is a subject of much controversy in the UK. Some parents believe that advertising manipulates their children into wanting things they don't need, whilst others believe that advertising helps them to choose things their children will like.

M1 I understand some research has been carried out to determine what parents think about this. What does the research tell us?

F1 Yes. According to a report on the Promotion of Food to Children, published in 2001, there is actually little public concern over food advertising. Children understand that television commercials are designed to make them want products and this understanding is clearly apparent, even amongst the seven to nine year olds, the youngest children in the group discussions.

M1 I see. But do parents want stricter controls over advertising aimed at children?

F1 Surprisingly, no. Parents see no need for additional rules or laws regarding advertising. In a study in the year 2000, commissioned by the Advertising Education Forum, 86 per cent of parents did not mention TV advertising as one of the five major influences on their food choice. In the UK, only 5 per cent mentioned advertising as an influence, and in Denmark 41 per cent. In Sweden, where TV advertising to children is banned, 11 per cent of parents felt it to be a major influence.

M1 So, in general then, do parents and adults see advertising to children as a major problem?

F1 Not really, no. Across several studies of parental attitudes, there is general agreement that advertising is not one of the major influences on their children and that broadly parents, brothers and sisters, friends and school are more powerful.

M1 Margarita, does advertising have any effect on diet-related problems?

F1 Not really, no. For example, Norway and Belgium have three or four times less food advertisements per hour on average than Germany, Denmark, Finland and the Netherlands, yet suffer from higher levels of obesity. In Quebec, where advertising to children on TV has been banned for over 20 years, levels of obesity are no lower than in any other Canadian provinces.

M1 Is there any scientific evidence of the extent of advertising's influence on food choice?

F1 Most certainly, although it is difficult to come to any conclusions because the facts seem to contradict themselves.

M1 Can you give us an example?

F1 Well, in 2003 it was found that food advertising had an effect on children's preferences, buying behaviour and consumption. However, there is no reason to assume that advertising will negatively affect a child's dietary health. It can influence it, but this influence could just as easily be positive as negative.

M1 Yes, I can see that.

F1 Children today are exposed to a wider range of influences than any other generation. Restricting advertising during children's programming would not protect them from commercial messages. Understanding the role of marketing and developing the ability to make critical comparisons is an essential part of growing up and becoming a citizen in a free market democracy.

M1 Margarita, thank you for a very interesting and useful discussion. Now let's go to our reporter in …

Unit 5 (Track 2)

Listen to this interview about dangers in the home and complete the notes in your workbook. You will hear the interview twice.

M1 Good afternoon and welcome to 'Good Home'. My guest today is Corina Montero, a college lecturer who specialises in children's safety in the home.

F1 Hello.

M1 Corina, I would have thought that the home is the safest place for children to be!

F1 Well, yes, it should be, but there are unexpected dangers which we all need to be aware of!

M1 Dangers? In the home?

F1 Yes! Although most things in the home are safe, it is nonetheless important to note that safety is perhaps the most important life skill that children need to learn from an early age.

M1 You're joking!

F1 Unfortunately, I'm not. Most accidents in the home mainly happen in the living room, bedroom, on the stairs and in the kitchen. Falls accounts for the greatest number of accidents, followed by 'striking' accidents – that is, bumping into things, objects falling on feet, things like that.

M1 So presumably there are some basic guidelines for making the home a safer place for children?

F1 Yes, there are some simple rules which are easy to follow. First of all, chemicals and medicines are safe if used properly but can cause harm if swallowed so they need to be stored properly and out of reach. Secondly, electricity can be dangerous if used incorrectly.

M1 Yes, please tell us more about that, Corina.

F1 Well, overloading powerpoints with too many appliances, and not checking the condition of your electrical equipment is extremely dangerous.

M1 Everything you say is very obvious, isn't it?

F1 Oh yes, but people don't think an accident could happen to them.

M1 What other things should we be aware of?

F1 Well, a great many children have accidents involving fires. They should never play with matches and lighters, and if there's a bonfire in the garden, children should be supervised at all times.

M1 And of course it's important that they understand that fire is not a toy.

F1 Definitely. But not just fires – don't forget hot ovens and hot drinks! Hot drinks can scald up to half an hour after being made.

M1 Corina, thank you very much for pointing out some of the hazards which we, and particularly children, may face in the home. I for one will think twice next time I cook a meal.

Unit 9 (Track 3)

Listen to this interview with an Indian classical dancer and follow the instructions in your workbook. You will hear the interview twice.

M1 Good evening to our listeners and to our special guest this evening Dr Sinduri Jayasinghe, the famous Indian classical dancer.

F1 Good evening and thank you for inviting me.

M1 Now, Dr Sinduri, our listeners are waiting to hear about your career as a professional Indian classical dancer. What can you tell us?

F1 Well, it all started at the theatre, where I was born.

M1 You were born in a theatre?

F1 Yes! My mother was actually at the theatre watching a performance when she gave birth to me.

M1 How did you become interested in dancing?

F1 I started learning classical dance forms that originated in southern India at a very early age. I became famous when I danced the 'Arangetram', which is a very crucial performance for a dancer.

M1 Why is this dance, the Arangetram, so important?

F1 It is a special offering by the debutante to her teacher, family, friends and critics. The performance can have a great impact on the dancer's career, as the judgement of the critics is crucial. Fortunately, the response was extremely complimentary about me, and I was even raved about by the critics and media alike.

M1 What happened after that?

F1 Well, since then, I have had the unique distinction of making over 1,600 live performances, besides being one of the youngest dancers invited to dance at the prestigious residence of the President of India. Also, I am a graduate from the Madras Music College and I was selected best dancer of Tamil Nadu state in 1984.

M1 Tell us something about your training.

F1 Since the age of three, I have had intensive training from Mr Pillai, who is one of the leading dance gurus of India. His style of teaching includes history, theory, dance music, development and dance technique.

M1 What else do you do in your busy schedule?

F1 Well, I choreograph all of my own productions as well as dance programmes for other artists in different dance forms, such as Indian folk dances and many other traditional folk dances of India and Sri Lanka.

M1 Do you teach a particular age or ability?

F1 No. I love to teach dance to all those interested, irrespective of their age and ability. I particularly enjoy teaching children and the poor. I have been teaching girls from impoverished homes, for free, as my contribution to society.

M1 That is wonderful. Could you tell us something about your dance performances?

F1 Well, I have been an 'A' grade artist for over 10 years in Indian television. My performances have been televised a number of times on the 'National Programme of Music and Dance' and on regional programmes. As a young dancer I proved that I was capable of dancing solo for three hours at a stretch to an audience of dance connoisseurs. Also, I am the lead dancer of my own group of 60 performers. Since 1986 I have toured the United Kingdom, France, Germany, the former Soviet Union, Canada, Singapore, Malaysia, Japan and the USA. Finally, I am an artist for the 'Indian Council of Cultural Relations' of the Indian Government, which sends members throughout the world as goodwill ambassadors to promote Indian culture.

M1 Well, Dr Sinduri, that is certainly an amazing career. I would like to thank you on behalf of myself and our listeners for being with us today.

Unit 10 (Track 4)

Listen to this interview about a mathematical discovery and then answer the questions in your workbook. You will hear the interview twice.

M1 On this week's 'Science in Action' programme we welcome Professor Emilia Pavlida, a mathematics specialist. Good morning, professor.

F1 Good morning, Thomas.

M1 Professor can you tell us exactly what a prime number is?

F1 A prime number is any number which can only be divided by itself and 1, for example 5, 23 and 101.

M1 So … 9 would not be a prime number because it can be divided by 3, as well as by itself and 1?

F1 That's right.

M1 So why are they so important? What is all the fuss about?

F1 Primes are important to mathematicians because they help in the study of codes, which has become an increasingly relevant topic with the rise in importance of the internet.

M1 So should I be using my spare time to find prime numbers?

F1 No, it would probably be a complete waste of time. The most recently discovered prime number was over four million digits in length and …

M1 I'm sorry, did you say over four million digits in length?

F1 Yes! There are computers searching 24 hours a day to find the next biggest prime. In the time it would take you to write out four million digits, say three weeks, another prime might have been found!

M1 Amazing!

F1 And there are cash prizes to be won by the person whose computer finds it!

M1 Cash prizes? How much money is being offered?

F1 There is a competition at the moment which is offering 100,000 dollars to the first person to find a 10 million digit prime number. A few years ago 50,000 dollars was awarded for the first million-digit prime number discovered.

M1 So who found the most recent biggest prime number?

F1 Well, there are more than 130,000 volunteers and their computers using special programs that examine different numbers to see whether they are prime. The latest 'largest prime' was discovered by a computer belonging to Michael Cameron, a 20-year-old Canadian. It took 45 days to find!

M1 So why was Mr Cameron searching for the prime?

F1 A friend had informed him that if he was going to leave his computer on all the time he should make use of it, so he put the software program on his computer. 45 days later his computer found the prime number.

M1 Professor, how many prime numbers are there, or don't we know?

F1 New primes are being discovered at the rate of about one a year, and we have no idea how many there are.

M1 And all I need is an internet connection and the special computer program?

F1 Yes, and a lot of patience!

M1 Profesor Pavlida, thank you very much for your time.

F1 You're welcome, and good luck in your search for the first 10 million digit prime number!

Unit 14 (Track 5)

Listen to this interview about the world's smallest lizard and answer the questions in your workbook. You will hear the interview twice.

F1 Good evening and welcome to 'The Animal Show'. Today we welcome Stefano Maloni, a conservationist who has recently returned from the Caribbean. Stefano, tell us about the amazing work that you are doing.

M1 Well, we've just discovered a lizard which lives on Isla Beata, a small, forest-covered island in the Caribbean. At just 16 millimetres from nose to tail, the Jaragua is the world's smallest lizard. It was discovered by us in three different sites and we believe that the lizard lives in only these areas.

F1 Why is finding this particular lizard so important?

M1 Because it's quite likely that the Jaragua is about as small as a land animal can be. There are about 23,000 species of reptiles, bird and mammal across the world. Smaller animals have a danger of dying out because of the small size of their bodies, as well as the minimum size needed for a functioning nervous system.

F1 Do you think the Jaragua is the smallest lizard out there?

M1 No, I don't. I think that there are other tiny lizards but the Jaragua will hold the record for some time. It's not likely that we'll encounter a smaller one in the near future.

F1 Are there any other small animals in the Caribbean?

M1 Yes, there are. The Caribbean is also home to the world's smallest bird, frog and snake. We think that these small animals could become popular environmental selling points, as they would appeal to children. It is very important to make people aware that only 10 per cent of the Caribbean's original forests remain, and a wave of extinction may soon hit the region. We're going to have losses, and it is only a matter of time.

F1 How do you feel about the future of the Caribbean?

M1 I feel optimistic about the Jaragua lizard because Isla Beata is part of a national park and local people have formed conservation organisations. The park's remoteness and ruggedness give it further protection. Of course, there are dangers for the lizard because of its size. Because it is so small it lives like an insect and feeds on other small insects. It must be on guard against being eaten by predators such as centipedes and scorpions.

F1 Stefano, thank you very much for joining us today. Good luck in the future with your environmental campaigns.

Unit 15 (Track 6)

Listen to the talk about the future of DVDs and then answer the questions from your workbook. You will hear the talk twice.

M1 To begin with, we had records: you know, those big black discs which got scratched so easily, but at least if one side was ruined, you could always play the other side! Then, in the late 1960s, audio cassettes became the thing to be seen with, and our roadsides became host to kilometre after kilometre of unwanted brown tape. There were video cassettes as well, and they seem to have survived better than their audio counterparts. Next, about twenty years on, in the early 1990s, compact discs, or CDs to you and me, arrived. At greater expense, of course, and they have been around ever since. But soon they too are going to disappear without a trace, just as records and cassettes have done.

Recently arrived, and still somewhat unknown and misunderstood by many people, is the DVD. It looks exactly like the CDs you insert in your computer at home or work. DVDs are quickly destroying video, which could soon become completely obsolete. Now, experts in the music industry are predicting that within the next ten years, DVD A (A stands for 'audio') will have done the same to CDs.

So, what are the advantages of using DVDs? Well, firstly, instead of playing in only two tracks (stereo), a DVD can play in six, giving you as close to 'pure sound' as is currently possible. This advance in sound quality is far greater than when we moved from cassette to CD. The difference is amazing. Secondly, the amount of storage space is very important. A single DVD is capable of holding more than 8 times the information that a normal CD can; if you 'layer' them (put two DVDs one on top of the other in one disc), this increases the capacity even more. If you remove moving pictures from a DVD (about 95 per cent of the storage on a DVD video is pictures), the space for sound is vast. A DVD audio book could hold the entire Harry Potter series.

But as always, there are drawbacks as well. A DVD will not play in any equipment other than that specified as a DVD player – in other words, unfortunately, you can't play a DVD in a CD player. So that means a lot of extra expense because you'll need a new DVD player for films, another one for your sound system, another one in the car, a personal player for when you go jogging, and so on. Also, currently, the facility to record on a DVD is still quite primitive and, while DVD recorders are available, they are still relatively expensive.

Unit 19 (Track 7)

Listen to this interview with a Marketing Assistant in the fashion world and answer the questions from your workbook. You will hear the interview twice.

M1 Today on 'Fashion Plus' we're very pleased to welcome Natasha Kafouros, winner of this year's fashion marketing award. Natasha, tell us something about how you got your current job.

F1 Hello, Manuel. Well, I had always wanted to get into fashion and I applied for my first job when I saw a website advert. I was interviewed and got the job as PA to the Marketing Director in a large fashion company. Shortly after I started, a vacancy came up for the Marketing Assistant role in the same company, so I decided to try for it and got it!

M1 Why do you think you were so suitable for the job?

F1 Hmmm ... I had a lot of relevant work experience before I got this job, which helped me gain experience in the industry. Also, I was able to build up a large contacts list, which is really useful in the fashion business. I think that really helped me.

M1 How important was it that you went to university?

F1 It's very important to have a degree because it gives you lots of different skills that are vital in the working world.

M1 Such as?

F1 Well, communication skills, computer skills, and most importantly for my job, meeting deadlines!!

M1 What steps would you recommend to someone who wanted to go into the world of fashion?

F1 Firstly, get as much work experience as you can in lots of different areas of the industry, so you can see which part you want to go into. Definitely create a contact book and put absolutely everyone you meet in it – you never know when you might need them!

M1 That sounds like excellent advice. What else?

F1 Always be on the look out for jobs and opportunities. Spread the word that you are looking for something and make yourself invaluable during work experience so that people will remember you! The fashion industry is not as fickle as you may think ...

M1 What do you mean exactly?

F1 They know what they want and what they are looking for, so don't be scared to push your way in if you think you have what they want. The industry doesn't change easily. Don't be shy. It's much better to be confident because this is another excellent way of making people remember you.

M1 Natasha, what other advice can you give our listeners?

F1 Be open to all the different areas of fashion, for example public relations, styling, writing, marketing, buying, and so on. Try not to limit your options, especially at the beginning. And finally, read lots of fashion magazines because this will help you to stay 'on the pulse' and remain in touch with all aspects of the business.

Answers

Unit 1

Task 1

1

a number
b noun
c list of nouns
d noun
e a number
f action
g a name (proper noun)
h a name (proper noun)

3

ii because it provides all the information that is necessary

4

a Two
b A boat
c Four from: exotic plants, wild flowers, ancient cairns, crumbling castles, sparkling white sands and an azure sea.
d The Tropics
e 2,000
f Check times and tides for availability
g St Mary's
h St Agnes

Task 2

5

For example:
Ramps on pavements
Wide doors
Special toilets

7

Special drop-off/pick-up spaces
Parking
Special check-in counters and waiting areas
Toilets
First Aid
Free telephones and information desks

8

For example:
Passport control
Easy access to and through passport control for customers in wheelchairs

Shopping
Wide aisles in our shops for customers in wheelchairs and special low level tills/counters

Language focus

9

For example:

a <u>Whether</u> you go <u>or</u> not I want to go to the party.

b <u>Whether</u> he had worked harder <u>or</u> not he would not have passed the exams.

c 'Shall we go <u>whether</u> it rains <u>or</u> not?'

10

adjective	adjective opposite	noun	verb	adverb
beautiful	ugly	beauty	beautify	beautifully
exotic	familiar	exoticism	–	exotically
inhabited	uninhabited	habitation	inhabit	–
available	unavailable	availability	avail	–
commercial	–	commerce	commercialise	commercially
accessible	inaccessible	access	access	–
additional	–	addition	add	additionally
–	–	assistance	assist	–
medical	–	medication	medicate	medically
special	normal	specialist	specialise	specially

11

For example:

a That is the person who won the prize.

b These are the reasons why they left school.

c This is the team that won the championship.

12

a Regarded as one of the best on the African continent, this hotel has been voted the best in Zimbabwe.

b Starting with a meal cooked by our head chef, your evening continues with a programme of African music and dance.

c Offering a full range of 5* facilities, the hotel has its own cinema, as well as a pool complex with diving boards.

13

For example:

a Regarded as one of the best films ever made, it continues to attract viewers.

b Beginning with the lowest level, the students work themselves up to the top.

c Considered to be the best restaurant in town, it is always busy.

Unit 2

Task 1

1

The spread of the plague through Europe during the 14th century, showing where the plague was at different times.

2 & 3

a infection
b made sense of
c destroyed
d deadly
e germ
f causes
g unaffected by
h rats
i different types
j removed

4 & 5

a What is the name of the bacterium whose code has been <u>deciphered</u>?
b Apart from being resistant to drugs, what other <u>threat</u> does the bacterium pose to humans?
c When did the plague <u>first affect Europe</u>?
d <u>Where</u> does modern plague <u>survive today</u> and <u>how</u> is it <u>transferred to humans</u>?
e List <u>four other diseases</u> whose genetic codes have been deciphered by scientists.
f What effect did the 'Black Death' have on Europe in the <u>14th century</u>?
g In which <u>direction</u> did the plague <u>travel across Europe</u> in the 14th century?
h How was the <u>vet</u> <u>infected</u> with pneumonic plague?
i <u>What form</u> did the plague probably take <u>1,500</u> years ago?
j Name the <u>two varieties</u> of plague known to scientists.
k Why was bubonic plague originally called 'Pasteuralla pestis'?
l When and where were <u>855 people killed</u> by pneumonic plague?

6

a Yersinia pestis.
b As a chemical weapon in a war.
c In the 6th and 8th centuries.
d It survives in rodents and is transferred by an infected insect bite.
e Cholera, malaria, leprosy and meningitis.
f It wiped out one third of Europe's population.
g It spread westwards.
h An infected cat sneezed on him.
i Stomach infection.
j The lethal pneumonic variety and the bubonic variety.
k Named after Louis Pasteur.
l In India in 1992.

Task 2

7 & 8

a activities
b routine
c digging out
d complex
e legends
f careful
g community
h expedition
i discovered
j strength
k worried

The word in the shaded area is 'Argonauts'.

9

1. myths
2. excavating
3. settlement
4. perplexed
5. stumbled across
6. determination
7. exploits
8. mundane
9. painstaking
10. composite
11. quest

10

a. What have <u>archaeologists</u> <u>found</u> in central Greece?
b. What is the <u>shape</u> of a 'tholos'?
c. When was the <u>community</u> <u>first</u> <u>discovered</u>?
d. How did <u>Vasso Adrimi feel</u> when she examined the site?
e. <u>Who encouraged</u> Vasso in her search?
f. What has helped Ms Adrimi to <u>put together the evidence</u> she needs?
g. What does she think the <u>legend of Jason</u> may be <u>based on</u>?
h. Name <u>three items</u> made using the <u>moulds</u> which Ms Adrimi found.

11

a. The remains of what they believe is ancient Iolcus
b. A beehive shape
c. Nearly 25 years ago
d. Shock
e. Her professor
f. Modern technology
g. The exploits of a seafaring people who sailed on the Black Sea
h. Jewellery, weapons and tools

Language focus

12

a. deciphered / made sense of
b. destroyed / devastated
c. deadly / lethal
d. microbe
e. poses
f. resistant to
g. rats / rodents
h. strains
i. removed

13

For example:

a. The insects were <u>resistant</u> to the chemical and could not be killed.
b. The town was <u>devastated</u> after the bombing.
c. Rabbits are another form of <u>rodent</u>.

14

For example:

a. There are two types of wine: red and white. I prefer the <u>former</u>; my wife prefers the <u>latter</u>.
b. Both the <u>latter</u> and the <u>former</u> editions of this book are very good.
c. 'I think the <u>former</u> version of this film was better than the <u>latter</u>.'

15

a. The Solar System was formed by gases about 4,600 million years ago.

b The planet Earth was dominated by dinosaurs about 235 million years ago.

c Copper and gold were used by man during the Bronze Age.

d The bubonic plague was brought to Europe by rats around 1346.

e English was spoken by only 5 million people worldwide in the 16th century.

f Rubber was brought to Europe from Latin America in the 18th century.

g The radio was invented by Marconi in 1894.

h The first man, Yuri Gagarin, was launched into space in 1961.

i The Olympic Games were held in Athens, Greece, in 2004.

16

a World Health Organisation
b British Broadcasting Corporation
c Digital Video Decoder (or disk)
d Video Cassette Recorder
e United Nations International Children's Educational Fund
f North Atlantic Treaty Organisation
g Short Message Service
h Unidentified Flying Object

Unit 3

Task 1

1

absorption – process where something takes in something else

adequate – enough, sufficient

chronic – continuing for a long time

conform to – obey a rule

dairy foods – milk, cheese, butter, etc.

derived from – developed or coming from something else

free of – not containing

humane – not treating animals and people in a cruel way

poultry – meat from birds such as chicken and ducks

sparingly – only a little

strict – obeying all the rules

2

a poultry
b dairy foods
c derived from
d humane
e adequate
f strict
g free of
h conform to / chronic
i sparingly
j absorption

4

1 What is a vegan?
2 Why veganism?
3 Caring
4 Vegan nutrition
5 Protein
6 Fat
7 Vitamin D
8 Calcium
9 Zinc
10 Iron
11 For more information

Task 2

9

1 – b	4 – f
2 – e	5 – d
3 – c	6 – a

Language focus
11

spaghetti	hamburger
milk	kebab
goulash	pizza
honey	meat
sandwich	beans
rice	

12

advantages	disadvantages
For example:	*For example:*
One thing in its favour is …	A bad thing about it is …
A good thing is …	A point against it is …

13

For example:

a Once people used to walk everywhere; today they travel by car.

b Once only some children went to school; today they all go to school.

14

a Many vegans choose this lifestyle to promote a more humane and caring world, in addition to believing that they have a responsibility to try to do their best.

b A healthy and varied vegan diet includes fruits, vegetables and plenty of leafy greens in addition to whole grain products, nuts, seeds and legumes.

c In addition to being free of cholesterol, vegan diets are also generally low in fat.

d Calcium is found in dark green vegetables in addition to many other foods commonly eaten by vegans.

e In addition to 160 quick and easy recipes, *Simply Vegan* contains a complete discussion of vegan nutrition.

Unit 4
Task 1
1

1 a, d – understand the concept of advertising
2 c, g – children need to be exposed to advertising
3 h, i – children would suffer from restricting advertising
4 e – can influence requests
5 b, f – about food

2

a	impact	h	expenditure
b	intent	i	banned
c	persuasive	j	substantial
d	purchasers	k	pestering
e	insulate	l	influence
f	correlation	m	explicit
g	revenue		

3

a	false	e	true
b	true	f	false
c	true	g	true
d	false	h	false

Task 2

4

a – iv
b – vi
c – iii
d – v
e – ii
f – i

5

1 choose things
2 seven to nine year olds
3 86% of parents
4 TV advertising to children is banned
5 one of the major influences
6 three or four
7 negatively
8 critical comparisons

Language focus

6

contra – against
con – together, with

7

in – shows a negative, an opposite; in, on
ex – former and still living; out, from
ad – in the direction of; towards, to
pro – in favour of
en – to cause to become; make
per – thoroughly, very; through
sub – under

8

For example:

a A good thing is that they have the opportunity to be well educated; a bad thing is that many find that they would rather be out at work.
b On the plus side they are not taken advantage of; a drawback is that many families need the money.
c It is lovely to experience the change in the seasons, but people don't always like all the seasons.
d People need to be computer literate in our society.
   Not everybody can afford one so this leads to unfairness.
e Children need to exercise their bodies as it is healthy.
   Some children are not good at sports.

prefix	words from text	your words
con-	conclusion	conduct, convey
contra-	contradict	contraband, contrast
in-	investment	inequality, insufficient
ex-	exposed	extreme, exhaust
en-	encourage	enforce, endear
pro-	programme	prolong, protect
per-	persuasive	perform, perchance
ad-	advertisement	advise, adhere
sub-	substantial	subway, subject

9

adjective	noun	adverb	verb
childish	children	childishly	–
encouraging / encouraged	encouragement	encouragingly	encourage
developing / developed	development	–	develop
comprehensive	comprehension	comprehensively	comprehend
–	advertisement	–	advertise
productive	product	productively	produce
decisive	decision	decisively	decide
aware	awareness	–	–

10

positive – negative
partially – fully
minor – major
oldest – youngest
useless – useful
dissuasive – persuasive
narrower – wider
misinformed – informed
indirect – direct
small – substantial
specific – general
broaden – restrict

Unit 5

Exam Exercise 1

a They are exposing themselves to a range of potential hazards.
b As many as twenty per cent.
c Because of lack of sleep. / Because they spend so much time in front of video screens.
d Over 1,100.
e Six to eleven year olds.
f Repetitive movements and sleep deprivation.
g Overuse of games.
h Mouse elbow, video eyes, joystick digit, vibration finger and nerve trap.

Exam Exercise 2

a At 20.00 hours
b £255
c Two
d Restaurant
e Have an initial consultation
f Regular reviews
g State of the art machines and user-friendly equipment

Listening exercise

a life skill
b on the stairs
c Falls
d stored properly
e the condition of your electrical equipment
f Fires
g matches ... lighters
h ovens ... hot drinks
i scald

Unit 6

Task 1

2

a True
b False
c False
d True
e True
f True
g False
h True

4

a Children themselves
b Because they take away the natural ability to learn things
c When they see a change for the worse in their children
d Unhappy, angry people who can't communicate
e It makes children socially and academically ahead of schooled peers.
f Children mix with people who are the wrong sort for them.

Task 2

5

a academic
b salary
c short
d expenses
e initially
f contribute
g reputation
h graduate
i depend

7 & 8

c

9

a ...she knew she wanted to go to university
b ...she was worried that she would not be accepted by the other students
c ...everyone
d ...contribute to the home
e ...and saved nearly everything
f ...a good academic reputation
g ...of being left out
h ...there are many advantages to going to university

Language focus

11

Possible answers:

teaching – learning
hard – easy
wonderful – awful
often – rarely
recent – old
worse – better
artificial – natural
strong – weak
confident – shy
wide – narrow

12

university
pressure
interrupt
schoolyard
structured
siblings
concept
absolutely
encouragement
assisting

13

a siblings
b absolutely
c university
d assisting
e concept
f schoolyard
g encouragement
h structured
i interrupt
j pressure

14

a get off – get little punishment
b go in for – take part in something
c go for – try to get something
d point out – call attention to
e try out – test
f put out – extinguish

Unit 7

Task 1

1

a – 4   d – 3
b – 6   e – 5
c – 1   f – 2

2

a to do with the mouth
b destructive chemical change
c liquids for cleaning
d claimed
e stops
f prevents/stops
g soreness/swelling
h likely to be affected
i make better
j wrong ideas
k suggests/recommends
l tightening

3

Paragraph 1

Periodontal disease is the most common of all diseases.

Most people are aware of the basics of dental and oral health.

Paragraph 2

Xylitol is seen as the latest effective anti-plaque weapon.

It is seen as the most promising development since the introduction of fluoride.

Paragraph 3

Hyaluronic acid, which is found naturally in the gum and the eye, has been used to treat eyes after surgery and now is being used for gum health.

Paragraph 4

Halitosis plagues many people and is not caused by oral bacteria or from the stomach. Basic oral cleanliness can avoid this.

Paragraph 5

Another hazard for oral health is smoking.

Paragraph 6

Some nutrients, like vitamin C and calcium, are important for oral health.

Task 2

4 *Various answers possible*

a twice daily toothbrushing / regular flossing / dental checks / visits to the hygienist / low sugar intake

b anti-plaque and anti-caries (tooth decay) agent / related to sugar and extracted from birch wood / can't be converted to acid in the mouth / suppresses unfavourable mouth bacteria / inhibits plaque formation

c misconceptions that bad breath comes from the stomach or from sulphurous gases / brush and floss teeth and remove bacteria from mouth before breakfast

d citrus fruit, kiwi, strawberries, broccoli and cabbage / yoghurt, cheese, green leafy vegetable, nuts, seeds, canned sardines or salmon and bread

Language focus

5

a There is a film on at the cinema which I would like to see.

b A fireman is a person who loves his job.

c Is this the article in the newspaper that talks about the best hotels?

d Do you know the reason why they went on strike?

e Do you think they would forget the day that they got married?

f A cathedral is a place that is usually quiet and peaceful.

g That was the girl who passed all her exams.

h The carpenter is from a place which is a small island.

i Their craft is from a time when it was valued more than it is now.

j Wimbledon is a club where people play tennis.

6

a assume
b assertion
c bassinet
d passport
e cassette
f message
g massive
h tissue
i successful
j passive

7

a tissue
b massive
c passive
d assertion
e passport
f assume
g successful
h cassette
i message
j bassinet

8

a watchful
b menacing
c total
d accidental
e delicate
f dangerous – more dangerous – most dangerous
g crafts + man
  work + shop
  dress + making
  foot + steps
h very – highly
  sensitive – delicate
  wood – timber
  special – unique
  present – current

Unit 8

Task 2

3

1 I'm writing to let you know
2 I've never done
3 I like the idea of
4 I'd like to play
5 My idea is to
6 we could have
7 we never have much chance to
8 I think having
9 I hope that you will

Language focus

5

Br E	AmE
analyse	analyze
travelled	traveled
programme	program
cheque	check
labour	labor
theatre	theater
doughnut	donut
centre	center
metre	meter
gaol	jail
humour	humor
pyjamas	pajamas
honour	honor
catalogue	catalog
manoeuvre	maneuver
tyre	tire
practise (v) practice (n)	practice
aeroplane	airplane

6

a signature
b address
c dear
d informal
e sincerely
f faithfully
g formal
h date
i reply
j yours

7

a buzzy – lively and exciting
b click – press the button on a computer mouse
c tweenager – a child between the ages of 10 and 14
d retail therapy – the practice of shopping to make you feel happy

e attachment – a computer file appended to an email
f digital divide – division between those who have and those who don't have computers
g mobe – mobile phone
h adultescent – a middle-aged person associated with youth culture
i to format – to determine the size, shape and form of a written document
j cargo pants – loose-fitting cotton trousers with large pockets

8
a digital divide
b tweenager
c retail therapy
d adultescent
e attachment
f buzzy
g mobe
h click
i format
j cargo pants

Unit 9

Task 1

1
A famous traditional dancer who is now too old to dance

2
a line 10 – age new dancers are trained from
b line 12 – year Moiseyev was born
c line 13 – year Moiseyev was enrolled in a dance school
d line 15 – year Moiseyev formed a small company
e line 16 – year the dance group travelled abroad
f line 17 – year the dance group toured France and Britain
g line 25 – school founded
h line 26 – number of pupils who graduate
i line 26 – how often students graduate

3
a False   f True
b False   g False
c True   h True
d False   i False
e True   j False

4
b He first became a classical dancer at the Bolshoi Theatre.
d The best dancers are guaranteed a place in his dance group.
g He travelled abroad in 1945.
i He thinks that folk dance is overshadowed by pop culture.
j Every four years pupils graduate from the school.

Task 2

5 & 6
classical – traditional
crucial – vital
debutante – newcomer
critics – reporters
judgement – decision
raved – enthused
prestigious – important
choreography – dance composition
irrespective of – with no regard to
impoverished – poor
connoisseurs – experts
promote – support

Answers   119

7

a The Arangetram is the most crucial performance.
b A special offering by the debutante
c The judgement of the critics is crucial.
d Has the unique distinction of making over 1,600 live performances
e To dance at the prestigious residence of the President
f Leading dance gurus of India
g Different dance forms such as Indian folk dancing
h Enjoys teaching children and the poor
i She dances as her contribution to society.
j She has her own group of 60 performers.

8

a It is a special offering by the dancer to her teacher, family, friends and critics.
b It was extremely complimentary.
c She was one of the youngest dancers.
d History, theory, dance music development and dance technique
e Children and the poor
f Poverty
g Three hours
h Five from United Kingdom, France, Germany, USSR, Canada, Singapore, Malaysia, Japan and the USA

Language focus

9

has refused, has kept – present perfect
helped – past
continues, takes – present

10

The list below gives most of the many verbs in the text.

present	present perfect	past
continues	has refused	helped
takes part	has kept	said
think	has overshadowed	got
works		worked
says		enrolled
spends		moved
enjoys		was
trains		formed
needs		became
receives		toured
receive		recalled
says		admitted
graduate		cultivated

12

For example:

a We must win the race irrespective of how tired we feel.
b I am determined to complete the puzzle irrespective of how difficult it is.
c I want to go for a walk irrespective of the weather.
d We should go swimming irrespective of how warm the water will be.
e I think we should visit China irrespective of any problems with the language.

13

Unit 10

Exam Exercise 2

a It increases.

b About 40 kg.

c Benedictine monks.

d It is placed in a net-like bag and then into a mould.

e Each wheel of parmesan has its own personal air-conditioning system.

f Used as security for loans by banks / they increase in value as they mature / offer short-term financing for local people / for banks the cheese offers a very low security risk.

Exam Exercise 3

COURSE APPLICATION FORM

Name of your organisation: Instituto Acapulco

Address: 6 San Miguel de Allende, 1022 Mexico City, Mexico

Course required: Humanities

Total number of people: 28 students and 3 teachers

Duration of stay:

From: Saturday 18 June   To: Saturday 25 June

Student accommodation:

Male rooms: 6   Female rooms: 8

Activities for group (please tick):

☑ Swimming   ☐ Basketball   ☑ Sightseeing   ☑ Indoor games

Suggestions for other activities: Tennis / Shopping

Meal times:

Please delete times NOT required

Breakfast   ~~0700~~ 0800
Lunch   ~~1200~~ 1300
Dinner   1900 ~~2000~~

Special requests:

a Three people are vegans.

b One student is partially sighted and needs the course materials in large print.

c We are studying IGCSE South American geography.

Write a paragraph of about 60 words to briefly describe what type of programme would be most beneficial to your group

For example:

The course would need to be suitable for all the students depending on their different requirements. It should be a combination of studying and research but at the same time should also include activities which the students can enjoy so that they can relax and get to know each other outside the normal school environment.

Listening exercise

a They help in the study of codes.

b Over four million.

c Because by the time the prime has been written out another one will have been found.

d Discovery of the first million-digit prime number.

e 45 days

f He had use of a computer that was to be left on all day.

g We have no idea.

Unit 11

Task 1

1

- **A** deep sea diver
- **B** goldminer
- **C** steeplejack
- **D** forest fire fighter

2

- **a** perils/hazards
- **b** reduced
- **c** tremors
- **d** falling
- **e** soak/wet

Task 2

3

The North or South Poles *or* the Arctic or Antarctic

5

auroral – at the start of the day
devoted – dedicated
insomnia – sleeplessness
maintain – look after
motives – reasons
reigns – exists
swell – increase
tang – flavour

6

maintain   insomnia
reigns   tang
auroral   devoted
swell   motives

7

- **a** Cold and windy.
- **b** Winter lowest is –55°C and summer lowest –28°C.
- **c** They can't sleep.
- **d** They were crushed by ice.
- **e** Atmospheric pollution, sea level rise, climate change and geology.
- **f** Take warm clothes / be prepared to get little sleep / need to be sociable / be prepared to have a diet with little fresh fruit.

Language focus

8

- **a** determine > determined, determination, determiner
- **b** achieve > achievement, achieved
- **c** succeed > success, successful, successfully, successor
- **d** perish > perished, perishable, perishing
- **e** dissuade > dissuasive, dissuaded, dissuasively
- **f** explore > exploration, explorer, explored
- **g** isolate > isolation, isolated
- **h** climb > climber, climbed, climbing

9

- **a** successor
- **b** climbs
- **c** achieved
- **d** isolated
- **e** perishable
- **f** dissuaded
- **g** explorer
- **h** determined

10

adjective	comparative	superlative
tall	taller	tallest
thin	thinner	thinnest
cheap	cheaper	cheapest
good	better	best
bad	worse	worst
unhappy	unhappier	unhappiest
untidy	untidier	untidiest
clever	cleverer	cleverest
lonely	lonelier	loneliest
far	farther	farthest
much	more	most
shy	shyer	shyest

11

a longest
b heaviest
c longest
d greediest
e deepest
f most destructive
g oldest

Unit 12

Task 1

1

a innate
b pioneering
c profoundly
d distinct
e random

2

a the result of a baby just moving its jaw / it is an inborn rhythm vital for learning a language.
b normal, hearing babies / random hand movements made by all babies and 'silent babbling' using simple signs.
c with their hands / different from other hand movements.
d a lower more rhythmic activity
e could be used to help handicapped children to speak earlier.

Task 2

3 *Various responses possible*

Babies are born with a natural rhythm which helps them to develop their speaking patterns as they get older. It is believed that the results of this research will help children who have speaking problems themselves or are the children of parents who are deaf. It was thought that the sounds that babies make and their hand movements were merely random but it has now been proven that this is in fact a natural process in their development and one which guides and helps them to speak.

Language focus

4

a chameleon – French
b husky – Inuit
c quartz – German
d kindergarten – German
e thugs – Hindi
f sari – Hindi
g waltz – German
h chauffeur – French
i lieutenant – French
j rendezvous – French
k pretzels – German
l igloo – Inuit

5

chameleon	lizard	small lizard that can change its colour to match its surroundings
husky	dog	large working dog with thick hair that lives and works in cold climates
quartz	stone	hard mineral used for making watches and clocks
kindergarten	nursery	school for young children
thugs	violent men	violent men especially criminals
sari	Indian dress	a graceful dress especially worn by Hindu women
waltz	a dance	slow, formal dance performed in a ballroom
chauffeur	driver	a person employed to drive a car
lieutenant	military rank	an officer of low rank
rendezvous	to meet	meet at a certain time and place
pretzels	biscuits	hard, salty biscuits
igloo	ice house	house made of hard blocks of snow

6

a The tycoon was a millionaire by the time she was 22.
b The chimpanzee learnt how to count.
c This part of town is full of sleazy bars.
d She was wearing a long sable coat.
e Cocoa is used to make chocolate.
f The cosmonaut stepped out of her spaceship to loud applause.

Unit 13

Task 1

1

student A		student B	
weak	strong	weak	strong
No paragraphs Spelling Grammar Punctuation The article is too short Incorrect vocabulary use	Length of sentences Answers the question	Spelling	Correct number of words Good introduction and conclusion to article Written in an interesting way Punctuation Good grammatical structures

2

a Yes, in the second piece as it is directed at the reader and written in an interesting style.

b Yes, in both pieces but in the second there is a clear introductory paragraph as well as a concluding one.

c Yes, in both pieces there are mistakes in grammar, punctuation and spelling but the first is worse than the second. Spelling is a problem for both pieces but grammar and punctuation are more a problem for the first.

d Yes, in both the pieces, but in the second they are more clearly laid out.

e Yes, very much so.

Task 2

3

Student A

spaceship > the spaceship

offeres > offers

quick transporting > fast transport

peoples > people

by animals > on animals

nowdays > nowadays

it benefits to me > It would be a benefit to me

mars > Mars

in a very quick time > very quickly

people use to die > sometimes die

be able ever to pay a ticket > ever be able to buy a ticket

until I die > before I die

Student B

concidered > considered
comfortible > comfortable
mobil > mobile
youre > your
wich > which
becouse > because
messiges > messages
completly > completely
writting > writing

Language focus

5

a Meeting often is a good solution.
b Eating late is not good for the digestion.
c Going to sleep early is a healthy option.
d Assisting the old is beneficial to society.
e Saving money is a good investment.

8

verb	noun	adjective
establish	establishment	established
–	environment	environmental
activate	activity	active
direct	direction	direct
object	objective	objective
campaign	campaign	campaigning
participate	participant	participatory
train	trainer	trained
consume	consumer	consuming
investigate	investigation	investigative
equip	equipment	equipped

9

a consume
b objective
c trainer
d direct
e investigate
f equipment
g participatory
h campaign
i activity
j environment

10

a establishment
b environment
c activity
d direction
e objective
f campaign
g participant
h trainer
i consumer
j investigation
k equipment

Unit 14
Task 1
2

a rather large or fat
b doesn't behave in a grown-up way
c warm-blooded animal
d mainly Australian animal – female carries young in pouch
e barriers – things that hold something or someone back
f a kind of pocket or bag
g back
h continue to live

3

marsupial
mammal
immature
pouch
rear
obstacles
bulky
survive

4

a 5
b 2
c 6
d 1
e 4
f 3

5

a It represents progress.
b Wallabies.
c 2 cm long.
d In its mother's pouch.
e By using its thick tail.
f Walking or moving backwards easily.
g It rests in the shade.

Task 2
7

a – c   e – d
b – e   f – f
c – h   g – b
d – a   h – g

8

a It's the world's smallest lizard.
b The lizard was discovered in three different sites.
c Because it's as small as a land animal can be.
d No.
e Birds, frogs and snakes.
f Only 10% remains and some species of animal may soon become extinct.
g They have formed conservation organisations.
h Predators, which may eat it.

Language focus

10

				s	p	e	c	i	e	s	
					a	n	i	m	a	l	
c	o	n	s	e	r	v	a	t	i	o	n
					l	i	z	a	r	d	
				b	i	r	d				
				f	r	o	g				
					i	n	s	e	c	t	
					m	a	m	m	a	l	
				r	e	p	t	i	l	e	
				s	n	a	k	e			
					t	a	i	l			

11

a an offer
b an obligation
c past habit
d 'if' structure

12

a We should get up earlier.
b Every morning he would catch a bus to town.
c I should/would like to visit you next week.
d If I had the money I would buy a yacht.
e 'Would you like a lift?'

13

verb	past tense	past participle
a discover	discovered	discovered
b find	found	found
c have	had	had
d know	knew	known
e become	became	become
f say	said	said
g be	was	been
h cling	clung	clung
i compete	competed	competed
j take	took	taken
k feed	fed	fed

Unit 15

Exam Exercise 1

a The ancient cities of Petra in Jordan and the oases in Saudi Arabia

b Any time of the year

c In the city's National Museum

d $92

e Egypt

f Kenya and Gabon

g Hammamet, Tunisia

h Telephone or visit the website

Exam Exercise 2

a Outside front doors, on balconies and inside the home

b The right soil mix, a fertiliser and plenty of irrigation

c Books and the local garden centre

d The temperature

e Because of local climate conditions and local demand

f By its height

g Because they are not yet established

h Roots are loosened from the soil and leaves and branches may get knocked and broken.

i They provide a tropical atmosphere, they are tolerant of a wide range of interior conditions, they are practically maintenance free, they need only a little sunlight and a little water.

j They grow too much.

k No leaves to clear up and can grow very tall in a small area of land

Exam Exercise 4

a – did not exist as a separate continent
  – connected to South America and Australia

b – separation of continents began
  – it became isolated
  – land mammals began to populate all the continents of the world
  – trees suited to cooler temperatures flourished

c – densely forrested
  – trees died out
  – it became glaciated

d – covered by polar ice
  – fossils show plant and animal life
  – susceptible to earthquakes

Listening exercise

a If one side got scratched you could still use the other side.

b Video cassettes

c In the early 1990s

d If you 'layer' them and if you remove moving pictures

e A DVD will not play in any equipment other than that specified and it is not easy to record well on a DVD.

Unit 16

Task 1

2

public transport	places of interest	leisure activities	food
fare	Reichstag	clubs	cuisine
trams	Palace of Princesses	entertainment	eaterie
U-Bahn		shopping	tasty
S-Bahn	Olympic Stadium		restaurants

3

fare – line 8

Reichstag – line 22

clubs – line 3

cuisine – line 13

Palace of Princesses – line 25

trams – line 6

eaterie – line 11

U-Bahn – line 5

shopping – line 3

entertainment – line 18

S-Bahn – line 6

Olympic Stadium – line 20

tasty – line 13

restaurants – line 10

4

a U-Bahn, S-Bahn, trams
b Single fare ticket
c At midnight
d For the Olympic Games in 1936.
e In Bonn
f At 10.00 p.m.

Task 2

6

Architectural plans have been uncovered.

7

a – vi   f – iii
b – ii   g – viii
c – ix   h – vii
d – v   i – i
e – x   j – iv

8

a Variable-sized and outdoor.
b 180
c To save space
d Outdoor classrooms
e Adjusted according to the number in the group being taught
f A light and airy effect and using materials which will enhance the sunlight
g A positive impact
h 30 to 60 years

Language focus

9
a may not
b could
c must
d must not
e would
f might
g Should
h may

12
last – first
receiving – sending out
empty – packed out
retreat – advance
tiny – enormous
coming in – going out
informal – formal
same – opposite
shrinking – expanding
exactly – approximately

Unit 17
Task 1

4
a Fruit can reduce the risk of certain illnesses.
b Controlled consumption of starch is fine as it reduces fat and increases fibre.
c Snacks and sweets if limited shouldn't affect a balanced diet.
d Meat, fish and pulses are important sources of protein.
e Drinking enough water is a vital part of a healthy diet.
f Dairy products are essential for strong bones and healthy teeth.

Task 2

6
a significant
b low self-esteem
c peer pressure
d factors
e reluctant
f diagnosing
g body image
h self-conscious
i acknowledge
j genuine

7
a They are becoming much more aware of the warning signs. (paragraph 4)
b They also have to have a genuine desire … (paragraph 6)
c It is hard for a doctor to diagnose an eating disorder. (paragraph 3)
d Males face similar peer pressure … (paragraph 2)
e If a male has a well-muscled body …(paragraph 3)
f … significant increases. (paragraph 1)

8
a No government department or agency has collected any statistics.
b Low self-esteem
c Traditionally shy of talking about their problems
d Diagnose the diseases in males
e Increased public information and awareness
f They promote self-consciousness.
g Acknowledge and recognise the problems.

Language focus

9

Possible answers:

a Temperatures are higher this year, but in spite of this they are still below average for this time of year.

b He studied very hard. Nevertheless he failed to obtain the grade he needed.

c She worked very hard until late last night. However, she did not manage to finish off the project.

d In spite of filling the tank before they left, they ran out of petrol.

e People on the island are extremely friendly in spite of being quite cut off from the rest of the world.

f She speaks at least four languages. However, she is not fluent in any of them.

g His doctor told him to go on a strict diet. Nevertheless, he chose to ignore his advice.

h The team played very well all year. However, they didn't do so in their last match.

10

Possible answers:

fruit	dairy products	liquids	meat/fish	cereals
bananas	cheese	cola	beef	wheat
apples	milk	milk	lamb	corn
apricots	butter	water	cod	rice
pears	yoghurt	juice	shark	barley
mangoes	cream	squash	mutton	millet
papayas		tea		
pineapples		coffee		

12

a Bananas are not round.
b Chicken is poultry.
c Elephants don't live in cold climates.
d Cats are pets.
e China is not part of the same land mass.
f Drought has no water

13

a chicken   e bananas
b cat   f donkey
c beef   g droughts
d India   h penguin

Unit 18

Task 1

3

Girls play more of a participatory role than a passive one.

4

For example:

a Girls can't leave some tasks to boys.
b Girls are not distracted by boys.
c Girls do better academically.

6

a ... in maths, science and technology – lines 20–21
b They score 30% higher in tests – line 21
c ... fall during the middle school years – lines 3–5
d lowered teacher expectations – line 8
e Girls experience the freedom to speak out – line 14
f ... go on to college and ...– lines 22–23
g do not receive equal opportunities – lines 2–3
h fewer opportunities to participate – line 7

Task 2

7

a Read the question carefully.
b Make sure you follow the instructions.
c Look for the main points and key words of the question.
d Plan what you are going to write first.
e Make sure your answer is relevant to the question.
f Check the number of words you have written.

8

The second one because it first introduces the topic and prepares the reader for the contents of the article.

10

The first one because it considers both sides of the issue and comes to a conclusion.

Language focus

13

Possible answers:

a I'd rather I didn't have to lend you the money.
b I'd rather watch TV than go for a walk.
c I'd rather not eat anything now, sorry.
d I'd rather go to the cinema than to the theatre.
e I'd rather go on Monday as I am not so busy that day.
f I'd rather not speak actually.

14

A	B	C
huge shop	hypermarket	basement
come out	emerge	battered
unusual	exotic	emerge
doctor	surgeon	exotic
lucky	fortunate	flats
the jobless	unemployment	fortunate
apartments	flats	hopeless
cellar	basement	hypermarket
rules	regulations	regulations
piled	stacked	stacked
broken	battered	surgeon
impossible	hopeless	unemployment

15

Refer to Column C.

Unit 19

Task 1

3

c   a
g   e
h   b
f   d

Task 2

7

a – iii   f – ix
b – ii   g – iv
c – vii   h – i
d – v   i – viii
e – vi

8

a Where did the person being interviewed see the advert for the first job?
b What was the second job she applied for?
c What two things helped her get the second job?
d What three examples does she give of how going to university helped her?
e Why does she say work experience is important?
f What does she say you should always be on the look out for?
g What shouldn't you do when you begin a job?
h Why does she say reading magazines will help in your job?

9

a On a website
b Marketing assistant.
c A lot of relevant work experience and a large contacts list.
d Communication skills, computer skills and meeting deadlines.
e So you can see which part of the industry you want to go into.
f Jobs and opportunities.
g Limit your options.
h It will help you to keep in touch.

Language focus

12

a retailing – sale to a consumer
  buying – purchasing something with money
b marketing – promoting or advertising something before it is sold
  selling – offering something for money
c styling – giving something its own characteristics
  designing – creating the initial product
d career – a job you are trained for and plan to follow for the rest of your life
  job – something you do where earning a salary is the priority
e picture – could be printed, painted, drawn, etc.
  photograph – taken by a camera
f industry – general word used for an area of business in which a product is made or sold.
  factory – where a product is made
g shy – uncomfortable with other people
  nervous – frightened of a situation, or certain people, etc.
h confident – calm and unworried about people or situations
  brave – feeling strong about confronting a given situation

13

a		C	O	N	**F**	I	D	E	N	T		
b				C	**A**	R	E	E	R			
c					**S**	H	Y					
d				P	**H**	O	T	O	G	R	A	P	H
e		B	U	Y	**I**	N	G					
f	F	A	C	T	**O**	R	Y					
g					**N**	E	R	V	O	U	S		

14

a where the models walk during a show to display their clothes
b sophisticated
c extra things that are worn with the main outfit, e.g. shoes, belts, jewellery
d high-fashion industry
e clothes designed by a named designer
f style
g those who follow fashion very closely

Unit 20

Exam Exercise 1

a In the Eco class
b In the Eco organic gardens
c The amazing view of Carlstown and the river.
d Pay a small extra charge.
e – Special meals at reduced prices
 – Children under 8 are supervised in the Eco organic gardens
 – Eco class for children
f – Great choice of snacks and drinks
 – Wide range of vegetarian dishes
 – Access for wheelchair users
 – Large print food menus
g At 7.00 p.m.

Exam Exercise 2

a Because it is a refreshing change from the beach
b Opportunity to breathe in some clean air and enjoy the stunning views
c Hikers, bikers, nature lovers and skiers
d Because the slopes are not too demanding / slopes not long / excellent facilities
e On the western side of Cyprus
f Information on the trees, flowers and shrubs
g About 1,700 to 1,750 m
h Churches, monasteries and rustic mountain villages
i Archbishop Makarios III, the first president of Cyprus, was born there
j Cherries, plums, apples, grapes and pears
k Agros and Kakopetria
l Because of its tragic past, when it was hunted almost to extinction

Exam Exercise 3

Salalah Sports Day
Application Form

SECTION A – please complete in block capitals

Surname: ADALLAN   Initial: K.   Age 16

Male/~~Female~~ (please delete as appropriate)

Home address: 46 Ruwi Street, Muscat, Oman

Telephone: 246993   Email: kadilrunner@hotmail.com

SECTION B

Running experience & competitions entered: 100 and 200 metres
   Won Oman under-15 200 metre race two years ago
   Won inter-school 100 metre race for students

Name & address of proposed sponsor: Mrs Fatima Indiri, 719 Salalah Road, Muscat

Telephone: 246114   Email: Doesn't have one

SECTION C

Arrival date and time:	26 June at 06.00 am
Departure date and time:	28 June at 07.00 am
Do you require transport?	<u>YES</u> NO
Type of transport:	<u>bus</u> plane
Type of ticket (return / single):	return
Ticket price enclosed:	$15
Entry fee enclosed:	$28 <u>$45</u>
Do you require accommodation?	<u>YES</u> NO
Number of nights:	2
Special food requirements (please list):	none

Entertainment (please tick first and second choices):

27 June	☐ basketball	☑ film night	☐ beach walk	☑ exhibition
28 June	☐ volleyball	☑ exhibition	☐ shopping	☑ film night

SECTION D

Write **one** sentence of 12–20 telling words telling us why you think your application to join our sports day should be accepted.

For example:

It would inspire me to become a better athlete as I hope to represent my country abroad in international championships.

Exam Exercise 4

Possible answers:

a
- Whales also hunted by Europeans as well as by Eskimos and American Indians.
- Large fleets of whaling ships built when enormous value of whale products was realised.

b
- Over-whaling reduced numbers of whales rapidly.
- Blubber or fat could be dealt with at sea to prevent ships stopping frequently to offload supplies.

c
- The Pacific and Arctic Oceans became the new hunting grounds.
- The USA dominated the world industry.

d
- Helicopters, sonar and high-powered guns are used for hunting.
- On-board equipment and laboratories process whales in less than an hour.